The Professional Houseparent

The Professional Houseparent

By EVA BURMEISTER

New York and London
COLUMBIA UNIVERSITY PRESS

*The Field Foundation of New York and Chicago
generously provided funds toward the cost of
preparation and publication of this work.*

Preface: The Professional Houseparent

With our increased knowledge of the great emotional upheaval experienced by children separated from parents, there
follows the concern that the important work of the houseparent cannot and should not be attempted by untrained personnel. The word "professional," therefore, is used in the title
to convey the thought that there is a body of knowledge which
the well-qualified houseparent needs to have, and that basic to
his work of child care are certain methods, attitudes, and skills
necessary to do the work well.

It is in this connection that one hears more and more often
today the phrase "the professional houseparent." This is not
to say that professional understanding and insight, or an intellectual approach, take the place of the natural warm feelings
and capacities the worker may have for children, but rather
that a more structured training strengthens, gives depth to, and
enhances those intuitive abilities the houseparent brings to his
or her work.

This valuable staff member, who is responsible for the actual
day-by-day care of the child, is known by a variety of titles,
none of which is quite as apt or descriptive as we would like.
The term "houseparent" appears in the title because it is perhaps the one most commonly used at this particular time. But

at once we must explain that a houseparent may be less a substitute parent than he is many other things to the child, and that his primary focus is on the child and not on the house in which the group lives.

During the course of these chapters the various titles by which this worker is known will be used interchangeably. In America, we frequently hear the terms housemother, housefather, cottage parent, counselor, or child care worker. Nuns are usually called housemothers or group mothers. For the child, it is perhaps warmer, more simple and natural for him to say "She's my housemother," rather than "He—or she—is my child care worker, or counselor." In a number of European countries, where there are well-established courses for the child care worker, we find him referred to as houseparent, educateur, moniteur, group leader, Jugendleiter or Jugendleiterin.

Whatever the term whereby child care workers are known, the word "professional" represents an aspiration and a goal toward which they are discernibly and universally moving.

Acknowledgments

I would like to express my appreciation to the following friends and colleagues who, because of their unflagging interest in the foster care of children, gave graciously of their time to reading all or part of the manuscript, and who made many valuable suggestions: Greta Alder, Virginia Becker, Lotte Brunnschweiler, Vernon Daniels, Lucy Elmendorf, Franklin Gatland, Ellen Gibson, Reverend Benjamin A. Gjenvich, Helen Hagan, Anni Hofer, Robert Holzhauer, Paul Jacobs, Robert Mackreth, Erna Mader, Aileen Pinkerton, Marguerite Pohek, Clarence Ramsay, Marie Rohr, Dorothee Schuster, Monsignor Joseph P. Springob, Gretchen Stearns, Claire Stone, Margaret West, and the group who were members of the course for houseparents given at the Louis M. Rabinowitz School of Social Work at Hunter College, in the spring of 1959.

A special acknowledgment is owed to Dr. Bernhard Kaufman for his psychiatric consultation in connection with all of the material, and to Joan McQuary, of Columbia University Press, for her editorial help and direction.

Contents

Introduction: The Growth of the Normal Child

The child who lives in an institution is no different from any other child, but what has happened to him is, unfortunately, very different, and thus some of his needs are special needs. Before considering some of the ways in which we can help him, it might be well to review 1) the normal development of any child—the growth, steps, and phases he goes through, and 2) what it means to the child in placement, in regard to these developmental phases, when his relationship to his parents has been disturbed, often seriously disturbed. Some of the points to be discussed in connection with the emotional development of the child will come up again in later chapters. An attempt will be made here only to summarize (all too briefly) the general steps in the child's development.

From the very first, a baby needs the attention of the person who knows and loves him best, the one who is closest to him—his mother. A baby must feel that he is wanted and loved, that he belongs. His mother holding him, feeding him, talking and playing with him, coaxing a smile, is needed by him day in and day out. When he shows he is uncomfortable or in pain—hunger pangs or otherwise—and when his mother comes and eases the pain or discomfort, he gets a sense of her care and love. He responds with love for her. He soon recognizes her face and searches for it on awakening. The way she bathes him and touches him comes to have meaning for him. The principle people in his life are first his mother, and later his father and brothers and sisters.

When one observes a baby or small child in his own home with loving parents, together with visiting grandparents, aunts and uncles, it is amazing how much care, attention, and being played with he can absorb and relish. He enjoys the role of being a little king in his own household. As he grows increasingly sure of this love, care, and attention, his feelings of physical and emotional well being expand and deepen, giving him more and more a sense of security.

In contrast, the baby who is unwanted, or whose mother is deeply absorbed in her own personal problems, or troubled by marital, health, financial, or other burdens, may not be given the loving intimate care he needs. Or perhaps, a mother, left to raise a big family of children alone, who herself had a deprived childhood and later life, does not have enough within her to give each one in her large family the kind of maternal care which is every child's right. Sometimes, in a troubled household, a baby cries in hunger for long periods before he is fed. His cry expresses discomfort, frustration, anger, and hunger pangs, as well as fright. When such periods are repeated, they become the basis for a beginning insecurity.

Directly connected with the need for food and the satisfaction of being fed is the pleasure of sucking, an instinctive reflex with which nature provides the baby so that he will be able to suck milk from the breast or bottle. The sucking motions are such pleasurable sensations that the infant may continue to suck on his fist, even after he has been well fed and seems content. On the other hand the baby or small child may continue to resort to sucking when he is hungry, tired, fretful, and when he needs reassurance, seeking, within himself, the comfort that he does not receive from the environment. No attempt should be made to stop him from sucking, or to shame him, as this will not take care of the deeper feeling which may be bothering him and causing him to suck. It is his way of helping himself feel better for the moment, and if he is deprived of it, he will still do it in secret, or find another means to pacify himself.

A child passes from one growth phase to the next most successfully when the preceding phase has been satisfactory to him. If an earlier period, for instance, the one where being fed is an all-important factor, has left him wanting, he will cling to it, even as an adult. We find, in institutions, children of almost every age still sucking or wanting to eat all the time. Six-year-old David, the first of whose many placements began when he was eight months old, almost always had something in his hands to suck on, the corner of his pillow at night, a piece of cloth, or whatever was handy at the moment. Peter, at thirteen, weighed 150 pounds, wet his bed, and always sucked his thumb as he went to sleep. Vivian, fifteen, in a delinquency institution, sometimes filled a doll's bottle with milk and lay on her bed sucking it. Excessive need for food, a desire to suck on something, stem from this basic need for food and love, an emotional void which was unfulfilled. Or, to say it in another way, a continued craving to eat, smoke, drink, nibble, or suck on something may be due to an unsatisfactory baby life in general, when the child did not get the comfort, reassurance, care, and love during the time when he was so dependent on his mother to feed him.

As the child reaches the pre-school age, and during the years up to five or six, his world centers around his mother and father and the familiar boundaries of his house and yard. He teethes, he creeps, his parents help him with his first faltering steps and encourage him as he tries to walk. They teach him words, page through picture books with him. He trots after his mother in the house, plays with her clothes pins and pots and pans. The time comes when he asks questions and more questions. He has a real curiosity and he is learning to master. He dearly loves to touch, pick up, and examine all the small objects in the house within his reach. He tries all the doors, knobs, and handles. He wants to hold the spoon and feed himself even though he makes a mess of it. He develops the feeling, "I can do this, and I can do that." This is how he learns. His ego develops and his muscles and coordination grow. He gets praise, help, approval, his family is delighted with him and his efforts. He thrives on all this and on their pride in him, together with their encouragement and stimulation.

In his growth, he moves forward on three different fronts; his physical growth, his intellectual development, and his emotional life. These processes do not go along in three parallel lines, but rather they are closely interwoven, related, and dependent on one another. For instance, when the baby is fed by his mother, the milk she gives him is vital for his physical growth. But along with being fed, as he is held by the mother in a loving way, he also gets great emotional satisfaction from the warmth, comfort, and support of her arms around him. And when we consider the intellectual development, the striving to learn, this can move forward more naturally when the child is physically and emotionally secure and unworried.

Another important period in the child's development is his toilet training. This, in our culture, usually occurs during the second year; the muscles which the child needs to control bladder and bowels are not usually ready before the second year. There was a period some years back, when some mothers felt they were doing a fine thing for which they and the baby should be praised, when they had him trained (or "broken") during the first years, some beginning even at six months. We have learned now that this is not good. It is much better to let the baby be a baby, and to postpone toilet training until the time when the child is ready for it. The time differs with each child.

The baby absorbs much from the mother's attitude toward training. Now for the first time, the child has something by means of which *he* can exercise control of the mother. He can, and does, use the bowel movement as something whereby he can show his desire to please the mother, or by which he can fight, antagonize, and control her. The child's feces are not distasteful to him in any way, while the mother may indicate that they are to her. The child, having proudly produced them, and receiving praise from the mother for doing so, would like to keep, look at, and play with them for a while. Even smearing them is a pleasurable experience to him. When the cottage parent has a school-age child in care, who still wets and soils his clothing, and smears, or on the other hand, who is compulsively neat and orderly, these symptoms may be tied up with mistakes made during the period of his toilet training, such as too early or too rigid insistence of control on the part of the mother. Or the smearing may be an infantile phase to which he is still clinging, indicating that things were not right for him as a baby, not only in the area of toilet training, but in his life in general. Here the institution can be helpful to the child who is inclined to smear and mess about in offering substitutes such as clay, sand, paint, fingerpaints and the other materials mentioned in the chapter on play. The compulsive meticulous child, whose early training has inhibited him and made him fearful of getting dirty, can be made more comfortable too, when in the group he sees that it is acceptable to play with these materials.

When children are three, four, or five years old, they usually become interested in the difference between the sexes. The little girl becomes very much interested in her father, and the boy, in his mother. In fact, a sort of family romance develops, the little girl adoring her father, even imagining that she is grown up and will marry him. The mother may, at times, represent a rival for her affections, as a result of which the girl may have, from time to time, some unfriendly feelings toward her mother. The boy has similar feelings of wanting his mother to himself and the father out of the way. When the child has loving, consistent parents, the little girl also develops the desire to be like her mother, and she imitates her. One notices even the same intonations of voice in mother and daughter. The small girl likes to help with the housework in a miniature way, to do things like and with her mother. The boy imitates his father, thinks he would like to grow up to be like him. So although there are moments of resentment toward and rivalry with the parent of the same sex, there may be a developing desire of wanting to be like that parent. The child who grows normally out of this phase does so by identification with his own sex, and developing a strong affectional tie with the other sex. All children go through this phase, more or less, and it is not so difficult for them when their earlier experiences as infants and nursery-age children have been satisfactory and when both parents have been able to stand steady before the overly loving or overly angry feelings.

For youngsters who later come into placement, there may have been a disturbance of this phase, due to the fact that one parent (often the father) is not in the home, or because the parents represent people whom the child neither wants to fall in love with or to be like. Thus they need help after coming into placement. Here we are reminded again of the importance of men on institutional staffs, that is, maintenance men, house-fathers, recreation and group workers, as well as caseworkers. The boy who comes to an institution to live has rarely had a father or other man in his life after whom he would want to pattern. But girls, too, need men who represent a father figure, as well as being able to see and know happily married couples.

At six or so, the child, having been cared for in the fullest sense of the term, having absorbed a generous amount of warm mothering within his family home, together with the strong protective supportive presence of the father, has grown sure of his parents, his home, and himself. He has been helped to develop a sense of self-worth, of confidence, and of his own ability, within the familiar certain confines of his house, yard, and immediate neighborhood. Now he is ready to branch out in the world a little. But at this age, as at each age through adolescence, he needs to have and see both parents loving the children in the family, and loving one another. The child now likes to play with other children in the neighborhood, and he is ready to take on some new experiences outside the home, the greatest of which is going to school. There is an important new adult in his life, the teacher. The child's readiness to learn, his own participation in learning, his intellectual curiosity and interest in the world around him, depend to a great extent on how satisfactory his childhood adjustment has been up to this point. The youngster who has dependable parents, a solid home life, consistent care and normal growth, is much more eager to learn, and to apply himself to his school work, than is the one whose early care has been disturbed and unsatisfactory to him.

It is only at the approximate age of six and after that the child is naturally at an age where he can take on people and experiences outside the area of home and parents. Because of this, the principle is often followed that no child under six should be placed in an institution. The child under six who requires placement (unless his reactions and behavior are very severe) can better be helped in a foster home. Physically, emotionally, and socially he is not ready for group life. It is found, too, that children between the ages of approximately six and ten, or seven and eleven (there are no clear-cut age boundaries), get along in the group with less emotional upheaval or strain than is true of the child under six, or in the adolescent years. Many of them are able, during these years, to give themselves over enthusiastically and wholeheartedly to activities and to accept good adult leadership. They play hard and are able to lose themselves and become absorbed in what they are doing. Boys and girls like to play together. They are at an age, developmentally, when nature seems to give them a sort of a rest. But here again we find, with children whose earlier life was disturbed and uncertain, that they do not fall within the normal pattern. Instead of being out playing with the others, eight-year-old Kathy may not want to leave her housemother's side. She prefers to trot after the adult and be close to her as a two-year-old would. And nine-year-old Doug is always by himself, on the fringe of the group, playing alone with small-child toys, or absorbed in his own thoughts and daydreams.

Preadolescence is an elusive period, both as to definite age, and as to its characteristics. It has variously been referred to as a transitional period between childhood and adolescence, or a betwixt-and-between time, falling roughly from the ages of nine to ten through twelve. The child who, up to now, has had fairly good table manners, who kept his belongings in passable order, who was going along pretty well and not causing any particular concern, suddenly seems to be all at sixes and sevens. His table manners become messy, he scorns soap and water, he scatters clothes and toys, he does not hear or take in very much of what the adults around him have to say, he may daydream more than he did before, and he is generally more restless and unsettled. Good behavior may now be a thing of the past. It is as if something had stirred up some of his earlier less-desirable childhood behavior and habits. He is turning more to youngsters of his own age group and less to adults. He may have a spurt of physical growth, but not necessarily emotional growth. Girls are usually one or two years ahead of boys here. At this age, the houseparent often worries and seeks help in order to clarify whether this boy or girl is regressing, or are some of his new reactions, ways, and habits to be expected at this age?

It would be interesting if someone were to make a study to determine the comparative number of boys and girls who are at the preadolescent age at the time application is made for their care in institutions. Dr. Fritz Redl * says that most referrals to guidance clinics occur around this age. It may well be that there are numbers of children whose adjustment and welcome

* Fritz Redl, *Pre-Adolescents: What Makes Them Tick* (New York, Child Care Study Association of America, 19).

in family homes is precarious up to the age of eight or nine, and who, when they reach the less attractive preadolescent years, are not tolerated any more and are subsequently placed.

The boy or girl of this age offers a special challenge as to which group he should be placed in on admission or as he is moved from one group to another. Sometimes he is found to be the "big frog" in a group of younger boys or girls, and again, he may be the "little frog" in an adolescent group, not fitting in too well in either place.

Adolescence is a generally difficult period as houseparents of this age group well know. The boy or girl needs all the strengths, the good experiences, and the dependable relationships he has built up during a secure infancy and childhood to give him something to go on during the turbulent early teens. Even the youngster of adolescent age whose early years have gone fairly smoothly, whose parents have loved him and stood by him, may have an extremely trying time of it. And parents need all the patience, understanding, humor, and tolerance they can summon, in order to weather these years themselves. Even the most dependable, devoted parents will be resented at times. On occasion, the boy or girl may act embarrassed by parents. He lets them know that he thinks they humiliate and annoy him. They may come to feel that no matter how hard they try, from their teen-ager's point of view, everything they do or say is wrong. At other times this same adolescent will think that his parents are simply wonderful. Such swings in mood, in loyalties, in admiring or hating, of enthusiasms or denouncements are present, too, about other people and experiences.

During the adolescent years, the youngster is going through tremendous physical changes. There is a real spurt of physical growth and development. Boys and girls become increasingly interested in one another (girls earlier than boys) and what the adolescent's group thinks, and does, and decrees as acceptable, is much more important to him than what the adults around him think. One of the strongest characteristics of this period is the striving towards independence, and the beginning of severing parental ties.

The adolescent, rather than acting his own age, has swings, here, too. One day the fourteen-year-old wants to be eighteen and the next day he or she acts like a seven-year-old. The adolescent tries to cope with the present and its urges toward independence. When he cannot handle this, he may go back and act younger in order to re-live and enjoy some of his earlier experiences of which he was sure. Or he may, for a period, need his parents as a much younger child might (in spite of his sometimes huge size) and he is glad to know that they are there. This sure and certain past is something which the boy or girl in placement does not have. He may feel all the more torn between the unfulfilled need to be taken care of, to be mothered, and the desire to cast off all control and management, and to be on his own.

The adolescent is also bothered by extremes of mood, by irritability, unreasonableness, and may seem to be impulsively living off the top of his emotions. He rebels against many things, among them rules and restrictions, even though underneath he needs and wants limits. Life is disturbed and filled with complexities for the adolescent in his own home, even when he has secure childhood experiences to back him up, but his reactions are mild compared to the adolescent in placement. Not only is the adolescent in placement troubled by the usual characteristics of this period, but, in addition, all of the earlier disturbing happenings in his family situation and memories of the adults in his life who have let him down boil up again with a new intensity.

As we try to understand the adolescent who lives in the institution, it is important to know at what age the disruption of his home took place. And the actual breaking up of the home and placement of the child may have been preceded by years of living with the conditions that caused the final disintegration of the family. It is rare that a boy or girl is placed for the first time as an adolescent, or that he has had a stable home life up until that time. The case stories of one group of girls, all of adolescent age, living together in a residence for girls, were analyzed. Most of them had had repeated placements beginning as little girls, in foster homes, in other institutions, or back and forth to relatives' homes. Rarely had there been one sure dependable person in the life of the girl, no mother, father, aunt, foster parent, caseworker, who had been a consistent, always dependable, thread through her life. Rather, the lives of these girls revealed a series of broken relationships. Many had suffered maternal rejection, few had known a dependable father willing to support them and interested in them. No wonder they gave their houseparents a rugged time.

The teen-age boy or girl who comes into the group may cling longer and more closely to the adolescent world than do "outside" youngsters of this age whom the houseparent may have known. Adolescents generally, in their rebellion against adults, are an enthusiastic part of the adolescent world for a few years, but eventually they set up a more individual code of conduct and system of values, much of which they had earlier absorbed from their own parents and homes. In their later teen years, they tend to look upon their parents in a much more tolerant way and with a renewed appreciation. But in the case of most children who come to institutions the adult world has never given them warmth, security, or understanding, so they continue to rely on their own teen-age world to a greater extent than normal. Thus it is more difficult for them to accept adult leadership because they have not been in the habit of liking, accepting, or trusting it.

Only when a child is occasionally allowed some freedom of choice, a chance to decide a few things for himself, can he learn to make wise and thoughtful decisions. As with most things, he can best learn by doing. The institution staff needs to keep in mind those occassions, however minor, when the child, particularly the adolescent, can speak for himself. This can still be done within the limits set by adults and the overall rules. The youngster should feel that he has some say about the selection and purchase of his clothing, the size of the portion of food he is served, how he is going to spend his allowance, what he wants for Christmas or his birthday, and who his friends will be. He will make some mistakes, and hopefully profit by them. He may grudgingly take advice. If he does not get his own way, or has to give up something he planned to do, he will do a good deal of grumbling—and we let him grumble. Yet even when he fusses and stews, he is more comfortable with controls and adult authority than without them. But children are right in feeling that some institutions make too many arbitrary decisions for them and that they should be able to decide more things for themselves. And why not? Isn't the institution trying to prepare them for life outside?

Whether the youngsters in care are of adolescent age or younger, houseparents often comment on how impulsively the boys or girls act, how they are inclined to take what they want, and how they are willing to do only what they want to do, without much thought for the consequences or for the feeling of others. A boy or girl may defy the rules, be destructive of property or play materials, and not seem to care. The child who steals seems concerned only that he not be caught, rather than with the stealing itself. Thus it might be well to go back again at this point to consider how the child's conscience grows, how his understanding of acceptable behavior and his own desire to do the right thing a good part of the time develop.

The parents of a baby or young child, who love him and try to do their best as they raise him, begin to teach him early what he may do and what he may not do. The parent sets these limits because he cares for the child and cares what he does and what happens to him. A mother tells a two-year-old who persists in turning on the gas or electric stove, "No!" and she will perhaps need to tell him over and over. She may slap his hand to reinforce the point. But following this firm but rather harsh admonition, she may substitute an acceptable activity, one of his surplus toys which she has kept in hiding and produces when he needs something new to catch and hold his attention. Or, at this age, she buys a toy which has a series of bolts and small doors with various kinds of intriguing openings to divert him from and give him a substitute for exploring cupboards or refrigerators.

As a child grows older there are many, many times when he is told and taught what he may or may not do. He learns the limitations, and he not only needs, but is most comfortable with, adult control. He can make the best use of restrictions, of being taught what is acceptable behavior and what is not, when this is given to him by parents who at the same time are loving and who are giving him security in other ways. Ultimately and primarily the child learns out of a sense of love, that is, of being loved, and loving back. When he realizes that certain things which the parents insist on stem from their affection for him, their desire to protect him, and because they care, this has great meaning for him. At first, a child does what his mother directs when she is present and as she asks him. Later he does this—or conforms—when his mother is still in his presence, but now perhaps she does not have to tell him each time. Still later he learns to do what she has told him to do or expects of him even when she is not present. This is why it is so tremendously important that the child learn out of a sense of love, otherwise the child does not or cannot learn to absorb and make a part of his natural behavior and reactions this matter of limits. (Of course there can be overprotection too, and too rigid adult control, another story.) But if the parents do not care what the child does, when they leave him to shift for himself and he gets into trouble, then often strangers, such as the police, take into their hands his behavior and the punishment for it. When he is punished in an impersonal or punitive way, his subsequent behavior may be determined not by what is right or wrong, but by what he can get by with, without being caught.

The young child learns, not only by what the parents teach him, but also by the example they set for him. During the time when the small boy is resolving his feelings that his father is a rival for the mother's love and the little girl feels that she would at times like to have her father to herself, he or she is also developing feelings of being like or patterning himself after the parent of the same sex. The boy, in wanting to be like father, grows up imitating his actions, his behavior, sometimes his very mannerisms, often even later planning to follow his same vocation. In other words, he often sets up the parent as a sort of ego ideal or model. He will, of course, have periods of defiance, and will, from time to time, do things he very well knows he should not have done. But on the whole, he will go along in the pattern which the parents have set, and which they demonstrate in their own behavior. He will learn and live by the moral and ethical values his father and mother follow.

Such a developmental pattern cannot be established (and we see this all the time with children in placement) when there is a rejecting mother, or where the parents themselves flout the law, where there is severe and punitive punishment without love, where the father has either left the home or is not the kind of man a boy would like to be. Children who come from broken homes have often seen all extremes in adult behavior—excessive drinking, violent language, beatings, parents being unfaithful to one another, or trying to evade the law. How can the child's behavior and sense of values, then, be anything but distorted?

In the institution, which usually has firmly established principles of what is expected of the child and of what is expected of the staff in relation to the child, the houseparent usually has to start from scratch in setting behavior patterns which are reasonable and not too difficult for the child to attain, even over what may seem to be a long period of time. And as we mentioned elsewhere, it is much harder for a child to try to learn at eight what he should have had a chance to learn much earlier. And while it is of great importance for the natural parent to set an example of good behavior, it is all-important that the houseparent do so also. The youngster who has been neglected, abused, or otherwise let down by his own parents, may come into placement with the conviction that all adults are "phonies"—or whatever he chooses to call them. It is a long process for him to learn to trust and to believe that there are people who like and want him. The houseparent will have to set limits and some degree of control. But he is also in a good position to balance this with an attitude of acceptance, understanding, and giving toward the child. When a child's relationship to his houseparent has some real meaning to him, meaning which has been built up over a period of time (during which he has perhaps tested out the houseparent over and over again), and when a child likes his houseparent and is sure that the houseparent likes him, then he will try to do the right thing, part of the time at least, for the sake of his houseparent. And as he comes to know that his houseparent's discipline is fair, reasonable, and not punitive, he will develop a feeling for doing the right thing for its own sake.

1. The Valuable Houseparent

Miss Roberts had been a housemother for small boys in an institution while in her thirties and later she went into another kind of work. One day she was in a supermarket, pushing her cart, intent on her shopping list. Sorting out and arranging watermelons was a tall gangling boy of seventeen or so, who suddenly stopped with a watermelon poised in midair, and with a delighted flash of recognition, burst out, "You're Miss **Roberts**, aren't you?" Then he announced loudly and with **real** pride to the boy with whom he was working, "This is Miss Roberts, she used to be *my housemother!*" Both the other boy and the nearby customers who overheard with interest were a little puzzled as to what a housemother was, but the pleasure of Freddie's recognition of her gave Miss Roberts a heart-warming moment. Thoughts of Freddie, and his group came back to her again that day, thoughts of what those little boys meant to her, what she may have meant to them. It was reassuring that nearly ten years later Freddie remembered her with such a spontaneous burst of pleasure.

A cottage couple who served for many years in a large agency caring for delinquent boys had a large glass-topped desk in the little office alcove near the entrance to their cottage. Under the glass was a display of snapshots of sailors, soldiers, a marine with his girl, couples with small children, all of which had been sent back by boys who had lived in this cottage earlier. Mr. and Mrs. G. carried on a large correspondence, particularly with boys in the services, who had no one else to write to them. This visible reminder of the young men who were now useful members of society, together with their still boyish need for attention and continued contact, particularly when they were way off in Korea, Germany or elsewhere was a real source of pride to this cottage couple.

The boys and girls living in institutions have missed the most important thing which every child needs in order to grow up to be a fairly happy individual, and that is parents who love him and who love one another. Houseparents going into the work for the first time sometimes expect that the child who comes from an unloving and later broken home, will be grateful, responsive, and affectionate with a person who would like to take care of him in a good kindly way. It is often a shock and a disappointment to find that this is not true, and that the children are hostile, angry, and insolent. The language and intense feelings with which they express themselves can be pretty strong. Behavior may be most unusual, even bizarre, and not within the previous experience of the houseparent. As he learns more about the work, he comes to understand that these bitter feelings and the expressions of them are usually due to the happenings in the child's earlier life and the years of living under stress and tensions, leading to the final step of separation from home, and placement. "The human being whose needs are not met when he comes into the world, who is an unwelcome addition to the family, who is neglected, and who lives in an environment that is indifferent and cold toward him will develop hostility, resentment, hate, pessimism—all of which makes it very difficult for him to function." * To understand intel-

* O. Spurgeon English and Gerald H. J. Pearson, *The Emotional Problems of Living* (New York, Norton, 1945), p. 12.

lectually why this behavior is not unusual when one considers all that a youngster may have gone through is one thing; to live with a highly emotionally charged group of ten or more is another.

Results are often slow, and together with halting progress, there are usually many regressions. The houseparent has to be content with small successes, and even with a slight degree of improvement, often not as much, or as soon, as was hoped for. When a boy or girl reaches the point of going along fairly smoothly, able to make good relationships with members of the staff and other children, and is getting to be fun to live with, even being of some help as an "old" boy or girl, then also, he is ready to live in a family home again. The houseparent has to let him go; in fact, sometimes helps him to go, and in his place takes another new upset one and begins all over again. The housemother and housefather have to take a good deal that is negative, and to try to give out day after day much that is positive. They are dealing with emotions, many of them negative ones. This is more difficult than when one deals with things, or performs a more mechanical work, such as typing or working in an office.

The work is difficult too because of some of the reactions stirred up within the child welfare worker by the very nature of the work itself. The cottage parent is living and working with boys and girls who confront him with the whole gamut of psychological stress, tension, anxieties, and strenuous behavior in relation to past and present experiences and people. The struggles and symptoms of emotional conflict are in evidence in one way or another, daily and continuously. The worker may or may not be aware that some children, or some behavior, or certain happenings, or constantly living with upset children makes him uncomfortable and perhaps does not bring out the best in him. This in turn causes tension and fatigue, often the inability to tolerate the job, and the seeking of a change. The safeguard in all of this is that the cottage parent be given some help when his own feelings are stirred up and get in the way of what is best for the children. Such understanding can be deepened during supervisory conferences, in staff meetings, psychiatric consultations, and through study groups and reading.

It is helpful to the child care worker nowadays that boards of directors, together with executives, no longer expect an outward show of good, obedient, conforming children, nor the extreme old-fashioned orderliness for which institutions have been so rightly criticized. Rather, the aim today is to have children living as comfortably as possible amidst the clutter of the collections, possessions, and playthings which usually surround active youngsters. The cottage parent will have disciplinary problems daily. Sometimes the group will go along pretty well; other times it will be all off key. Individual children will often have bad days and difficult hours. By the very nature and composition of the group, this cannot be expected to be a smoothly running operation. The houseparent will have trying hours and difficult days, periods which will tax all of his physical and emotional resources. The child care worker will not always be able to show affection, understanding, and acceptance of each child, or at times, to the group. For houseparents are human beings and so they become angry, upset, and reach the end of their patience. Sometimes these feelings are provoked by the child who is so exasperating that his behavior and actions reach the point where they are indeed hard for the houseparent to take, as they would be, for anyone. Or, reactions may be aroused within the adult himself which makes it difficult to be patient with a certain child or a particular type of behavior. The best thing for the houseparent to do in such a case is to face his feelings honestly and to talk them over with the case-worker, the supervisor of home or cottage life, or other members of the staff who confer with the houseparent in a supervisory way.

Recognizing the grave and important work for which the cottage parent has been asked to be responsible, what does he have to work with, what are his tools? The child care worker has, first of all, his or her common sense, practical experience, intuition, and the particular flair for children, and interest in them which attracted him to this kind of a setting. We used to think that this was enough to do the job. But today it is seen that in addition to the group leader's own way of working, he needs certain available knowledge to supplement his native understanding of how to help a boy or girl in the group. And while common sense and intuition alone are not enough, neither will book knowledge of children suffice. The houseparent who himself had a fairly happy, normal childhood, followed by later positive experiences with children as a camp counselor, or with his own children, for example, brings something of this to those youngsters with whom he later works. Some ingredients of all of these factors are desirable: the experience of having been a secure child, adolescent, and adult; a firsthand knowledge of children; a liking for young people and a desire to serve them; and finally, a more disciplined study and knowledge that are a part of the preparation for this work as they are for any profession.

A second tool which the houseparent works with is the group itself. The way of group living has inherent in it factors which can be used in a positive way to help certain children.

And within the group, the cottage parent has something else to help him, the values and possibilities of which are all too often overlooked. This is the process of daily living, often referred to in a dull and prosaic way as "the routine." And while it has been true in the past that the daily routine was too often rigid and uninspired, we have now learned and experienced that it can be otherwise. The processes of daily living which the cottage parent and the group share can be managed, enriched, and used in such a way as to be healing and emotionally nourishing.

Another important thing which the houseparent has to work with is his or her relationship to the child. At one time or another, almost every houseparent must have asked himself, "What do I mean to this boy; this girl? How does he see me? What does he want of me, need from me?" To work toward the growth of a relationship which the child will learn he can trust and depend on, and using this relationship to help him, is one of the most important goals of the child care worker. Elliott Studt mentions, in connection with group living: "When we are working with a child whose ability to relate is so underdeveloped or damaged that he cannot at once use family living for growth, then we have to find some way of providing him with relationships which will help him begin to attach the business of living to positive personal experiences with human beings." * Relationships which are built on a firm, sound basis, these "positive personal experiences with human beings," strengthen and deepen with time, and often it takes months and years of time. This suggests the importance of continuity and a minimum of change within the houseparent staff. The whole

* Elliott Studt, "Therapeutic Factors in Group Living," *Child Welfare* (January 1956).

plan of treatment and care will be jeopardized when there is a high rate of turnover in the houseparent group, representing a series of broken relationships.

This job which has its difficulties, its methods, its tools, also has its satisfactions. Those who have been in the work for some time experience as one of the greatest of these the return visits of some of the boys and girls who have left, and who come back to tell how they are getting along, to show that they are doing well, often to bring the young man or woman whom they plan to marry, or the new baby. Sometimes they just want to see how the old place looks, to test memories, after having been out in the world, and to see if some of the staff whom they knew are still there. It is often at the time of some important step in his life, such as graduation from high school, the first job, entering the service, an engagement or marriage that brings the boy or girl to visit a former houseparent, or sends a letter or an announcement. Sometimes a young man or woman who is doing well may return and ask, "I was really quite difficult when I was with you, wasn't I," needing the reassurance that he was just a troubled youngster at the time, going through an experience trying for any child, and that the negative behavior or reactions were not unusual.

It is true, of course, that it is the boy or girl who has experienced success who returns more often than the one who has been in further trouble. But the houseparent often hears, too, about those who have not done so well. However, there are enough successes to give the child care worker something to go on. One housemother who had twelve years of experience put it this way, "When the going is difficult with my group, I think back to those who were with me five, six, or seven years ago, and realize that an encouraging number of them have done well. I remember what hard times they had as adolescents, but that they did respond to help, and this gives me encouragement as I work with my present group."

Another housemother was seated in a bus one winter day. "Suddenly," she said, "here was somebody giving me a poke on the shoulder and I looked around and it was Moira, now eighteen." Moira had been one of a group of ten for whom this housemother had been the relief worker five years previously. After a few words of visiting, Moira pointed to the knitted ski cap she was wearing, and said, "Remember? I'm still wearing it." This housemother always had some pick-up knitting as she sat with the girls, watching television or when she waited for them to come in on the nights they had permission to stay out late. One winter she made a ski cap for each of them, in ten different colors and patterns; another Christmas it was mucklucks.

There are many other on-the-job satisfactions, bits of progress and improvement here and there. An undernourished child gains weight, another child may cease to be bothered by nightmares and be able to sleep more peacefully, a third may show improved school interest and grades. Then there is the formerly disinterested youngster who suddenly becomes absorbed in an activity and cannot wait to resume it, or the child who learns to ride a bicycle and feels he is good at something. The housemother sees the beam in the face of the little girl or boy who experiences the first birthday cake with candles and presents that he ever had. There are the first fleeting tentative overtures toward a relationship, when John dares to trust an adult, when the housefather begins to reach the boy who has always put up a barrier, letting no one near him . . . Steve has not run away for a month now . . . it is good to hear

Michael laugh out loud with genuine enjoyment and humor, rather than with derision . . . Chuck finally reaches the point where he can stand up for his own rights instead of being the group's scapegoat . . . the day comes when Lennie *offers* to help. And so we could go on. These things might not sound too impressive to those not close to the work, but such steps may represent real strides for a child, and often only the person who lives closely with the group realizes the importance of such minor or major steps forward.

Children do not usually give compliments freely, and the houseparent does not necessarily expect them to. The adolescent particularly, but the young child too, may be quite free with his criticisms, but the compliments, if they come at all, appear in a very roundabout and involved way. An example of this was the huge Mother's Day card made by a group of adolescent girls. On Saturday the girls busied themselves in the basement playroom almost all day, asking their housemother not to come in as they were working on a secret and a surprise. Revealed Sunday morning, the card really was a surprise. The girls had taken a large sheet of paper, four by six feet in size, and bordered it all around with three inches of crushed aluminum foil. Another border of bows and roses, made from pink crepe paper, added dash and flourish. One of the girls drew a row of eight figures, really characterizing with a suggestion of line here and there, the eight girls in the group. Then there was a printed letter, signed by each one, which read as follows:

"To our housemothers on Mother's Day: We may cause you trouble and give you heart failure when we sneak out, put our lights on at 12:00, try on skirts at 11:00 at night, steal your coffee and run down in the basement and drink it, burn holes in our bedspreads, play hookey from school, steal flowers from people's yards and then give them to you, but don't let this upset you. We know we're not angels all the time but you must admit we do have our good points. Since we all have family troubles, and some of us don't have mothers to send cards to, we decided to make an extra special one just for you two. From all of us Senior Girls. Happy Mother's Day."

Youngsters who have gone through harrowing experiences—as most of them have—show us time and again that many have the ability to bounce back to believe in adults once more and to gain something from the experiences and relationships as offered in the groups. There is a real challenge to this work of being a houseparent which comes with the opportunity to help each child to develop to the fullest his particular latent capacities, in other words, to help him become all that is in him to be. An attempt will be made during the course of this book to take apart and look at again, some of the seemingly simple and homely things that go into everyday living in the groups, and to see how they can be used to the fullest. As we consider all that the houseparent does, and is expected to do, during the course of a day, or week, it will be to see how he, or she, can squeeze every possible value out of play, clothing, work, meals, allowances, and all the daily processes of group living. These simple life situations and how they are managed by the houseparent can be utilized in ways which have real healing and growth values and great meaning in the life of the child.

2. *Living in a Group*

Sally, seventeen, who had spent several years in a group of ten girls, was about to leave. Feeling quite mellow about the agency at this point, she made this statement: "Nowhere else would you find such a collection of characters, but you sure can gain something from each one." Sally was expressing one of the positive values in group living. The child with problems, the one who feels different, whom no one else has wanted, and who feels that he has been kicked around here, there, and everywhere, should feel, when he comes into the institution and into the group, that "this is a place where they try to help you." Something in the atmosphere, in the surroundings "speaks" to him. When staff attitudes are those of acceptance of children, of understanding those who are unusual or different, the members of the groups will reflect this, some of it at least, in their attitude toward one another. A youngster may have the feeling that he is different, that his parents are different, that what has happened to him has happened to him alone. Now he sees that others are in the same situation, and that the staff has a matter-of-fact but helpful attitude about it.

Another value in the group setting is that here is a place, here are people, and here is a daily routine that can be depended on. Children who come to institutions usually have had so little that they could count on. In this new place they can, or should, be certain of the fact that they can stay and that they will not be put out, sure of the house, the houseparents, and the routine. The house, even though it may be an ugly old brick or stone building, still looks solid and permanent. The child is reassured by the fact that when he gets up in the morning and when he comes home from school at noon and in the afternoon, there will be an adult to receive him and to look after him. Many of the children, while still in their own homes, had to be on their own at too early an age. Perhaps a mother worked, and a boy or girl came home to fix his own lunch, or found an empty apartment after school and awaited a tired mother's return. In some instances of trouble between parents—fighting, drinking, psychological strains and stresses—the child stayed away, unable to face his life at home, delaying as long as he could his return to the house after school and at supper time. A child does not like to come into a home where there is trouble, or into empty rooms. When later he comes into the place where his group is, he knows that his own or the relief houseparent will be there.

The very regularity of the routine gives security—the three good meals a day, plus snacks, one's own bed, and that the way things were done yesterday are pretty much the way they will be done today and tomorrow. Bath nights for a child's group may be on Tuesdays and Fridays; bed linen and pajamas are changed on Friday; the cottage parent gives out allowances regularly on Saturday mornings. When a child is sick, the temperature is taken, he is put to bed and made comfortable, the nurse or doctor are consulted. And so, on and on. These many seemingly small and minor things can be counted on absolutely, and this gives support and reasurance. The fact that the boy or girl can be sure of what will happen is important, and also that he can be sure well in advance. For this reason the cottage parent needs to do a good deal of explaining to the group, in regard to arrangements, shifts in staff duty, and changes in routine. The new boy or girl, particularly, needs to know beforehand each time the regular houseparent has a day off due, and the name of the person who will take over. For all of the group at all times, it is good practice to tell them of the worker's vacation plans, dates of leaving and return, as well as any other unusual absences away from the group. These children have a great need to be aware of those things which might seem simple and obvious to the adult. When a new staff member comes in, when a rule is revised, even when something as pleasant as a party is planned, youngsters appreciate being on the inside. They do not like to be taken unaware, to be caught off-guard, or as they might say it, to have something put over on them.

Coming together three times a day for meals, working side by side, observing the same rules, sharing all phases of the routine as well as playing together, makes for a growing closeness in relationships which becomes a positive group factor. In spite of differences, competitiveness, and rivalries within the group, the child usually develops a feeling of belonging with and a loyalty to these other boys or girls with whom he shares so much. The youngster, more often than not, thinks of his group positively, and with a sense of identity with it, even when he has some not-so-friendly things to say about individuals in the group, about the institution, and at times, about his houseparent. The new child coming in, who may have been hurt and rejected by the adults in his life, often turns first to the play equipment, the pets, and to the other children, and his relationships to them begin to take hold before he begins to trust a closer relationship with the cottage parent. Adolescents count heavily on one another for support. They may feel that no one understands, other than those of their own age group. It is of the utmost importance to the adolescent, in his own home or not, to have a place in a group, with others who talk his own language.

In addition to the other boys or girls, the child is exposed to a variety of possible staff relationships within the total setting. Many adults may be concerned with each child's welfare in one way or another. In addition to his cottage parents, he may have an uninterrupted hour or half hour with his caseworker each week; then there is his relief houseparent, the counselors of other groups, and the supervisor of cottage life. An adolescent girl may look across the campus with great admiration at a young male recreation worker, or the new housefather of the senior boys. Contacts may be only of a "Hi, Bill," "Hi, Jean," nature, as they meet in passing. But the friendliness of the young man, together with his respect for the girl may be quite a new experience for her. The boy or girl, in his casual or close contacts, usually finds one or two people whom he latches onto particularly. Some children seek out recognition and attention from many on the staff, others are content with less. The nature of the relationship is important, be it the close one with the cottage parent, or twelve-year-old Jane's crush on the swim instructor, or the companionship of overweight Jerry with the plump cook from whom he not only wangles extra desserts, but with whom he likes to talk over many of the happenings in his daily life.

Another of the positive values in group living is that there are many chances for each child to be given opportunities for successful accomplishments and recognition. This may be in some area of play, in learning to make his own bed, or bringing home a report card showing improvement. The house-parent, aware of the great need each child has to feel that he is good at something, makes more of the small things which he tries to do well, and gives recognition for bits of progress which might be overlooked or taken for granted in another setting.

Rules are easier for a boy or girl to take when he is a member of a group and they apply to all alike. When the new youngster comes into the group, the routines, rules, and the way things are done, are already all set and in operation, and the individual is more apt to go along with them than he would be if each situation where he needed some special permission were decided separately and individually, thus perhaps becoming a basis for disagreement between the adult and the youth. If the climate is good, with most of the members going along with the leader to a reasonable degree, then the new one coming in will take his cues from the others. He is not so likely to wage an individual war against what the others, who have been there longer, accept as reasonable.

One of the questions that often arises is the extent to which the individual boy or girl is expected to share with the others in his group, for example, when a child receives candy, fruit, cookies, or something of the sort from relatives. A housemother may wonder whether this is not a good time to teach the child to be unselfish and to divide his gift with others. Actually, this is not the time nor way to help a youngster develop these values. In the first place, until they reach a certain age, all children are naturally selfish. This is particularly true of those in placement who have received too little of the really important things in life and who are thus all the more inclined to hang on to the little material tokens of parental attention. The candy or cookies are to the child tangible evidence of recognition by his parents. He needs such gifts to reassure himself and even to impress others, and in most cases, he needs them all to himself. There is already so much that a child in a group is expected to share, including the cottage parents and many other parts of his daily life. He has little enough that is his alone, and thus those gifts which he receives from outside the institution should be his to use how and when he chooses without being made to feel guilty about it, even if they seem an overabundance for one.

This, of course, raises the question: what about the child who never receives anything from anyone outside the agency, either because his parents do not give to him, or because he may not have parents in the picture? It is usually with this child, who may stand by sadly and watch when another child gets a gift of good things to eat, that the houseparent expects the one who receives a gift to share. However, it would be better if the houseparent had on hand a supply of candy bars and other package treats that children cherish so, to use at the right moments for the child who gets no packages from relatives or elsewhere.

When there is a groupworker on the staff, he may enhance the values to the children which are inherent in the group structure by using, in a carefully planned way, situations in the daily processes of living, in order to help in the total care and treatment process. In this connection, Dorothy Kamstra, groupworker at Youth Services, Philadelphia, explains how the groupworker helps the houseparent gain "an awareness of the process within the group and some knowledge of ways to help the process be a tool for helping the individual. . . . Through the group experience in Youth Services they [the girls] have had an opportunity to learn to relate to others, to test their social skills, to find out what kind of persons they are. Any achievements they may have made in these areas did not happen by accident. We meant for it to happen through the awareness and help of the staff who use the relationships between the girls themselves and through program as well as their own relationship to each girl."

As the positive factors in group living are considered, we find that these values are stronger when the child has chances to escape regularly from constant group living, and to be by himself for periods. Almost everyone has the desire to be alone at times, and children need this, too. This is easier to manage in the institution which has cottages, with sleeping rooms for one or two. Then a boy or girl can close a door (or slam it in anger against everyone) and have some time and a place for himself. Sometimes when such periods of being alone would be quite possible, even in a dormitory setting, this is denied the child, for two reasons in particular: 1) that certain areas are "off-limits" during the day time, most often the sleeping rooms. There are still to be found the rule that children are not permitted in their sleeping rooms at times other than bedtime; 2) that it is more difficult to supervise a scattered group than one where all of the members are together. For example, the youngster who finishes his meal before the others at his table might want to go off by himself and play, or go sit on his bed and read a comic. This he may not do because of the requirement that all of the children at the table wait until everyone is finished. The cottage parent may be afraid that something will happen if one of the group, or several, are off by themselves. Too often a child is swept abruptly along with the group, and not allowed a choice as to what he wants to do, or to go to a part of the cottage or unit where he could be alone for a while.

It is true that the cottage parent will need to do more circulating, particularly when a greater freedom is first permitted, but this plan has been found to be workable, giving group members the much-needed respite from the constant presence of others around them.

Individualization

Institutions have come a long way in accepting for care children who present a wide range of personality and behavior problems. In connection with intake, many groups have certainly stretched a point in giving a welcome to the "unplaceable" child. But has this willingness to make a place for the individual—no matter if his history presents every challenge in child care—been matched by an equal effort to make use of all of the possibilities for individualization within the group? For example: study hall—is it required for a definite period for *all* children in a group, including Sara, who gets very good grades and is able to do all of her preparation in school or in a short time at home, and including Al, who is so troubled about so many things that he actually just sits at a table during study hall and doesn't accomplish a thing? Bedtime—must it be the same for all members of the group, or can some go earlier, some later, depending on their ages and needs? Allowances—can each child spend his allowance pretty much as he pleases? Meals—is the child free, as the adult serves his plate, to say he'd like a large amount of mashed potatoes and just a few peas? Work—is Mary allowed to go out baby sitting at fifteen, while Betty, who is sixteen, is not yet ready to do so?

A houseparent might say here, "Yes, but if I gave a girl permission to leave the table early she might go into the dormitory and rummage through dressers and closets and appropriate for herself some of the things she finds there. Or two boys in a dormitory alone might jump up and down on the beds or have a big noisy chase around the room, pushing beds and tables out of place as they go." The housemother still at the table with the rest of the group would have to leave and see what was causing all the racket. There will always be situations that will need to be straightened out after they happen, as a result of which it is to be hoped that something will be worked through, and that the chances that this same thing will happen again will be slightly less. We work toward the point where boys and girls can be given more and more responsibility for self-direction, but they acquire this only through practice, even if disciplinary problems and various complications come up along the way. Houseparents sometimes anticipate more difficulties than actually develop, and may tend to cling to the same arrangement and plan for everyone alike, feeling that life is easier and less complicated that way, as indeed it is for the adult, but this way is not the best plan for the individual child.

Individualization is carried out, too, in the amount of time and attention given by the group leader to each child. Some children want and need more, others less; it is never equally divided. Some children are more ready than others for closer, warmer relationships. The cottage parent feels and responds differently toward various children, and it is a good thing for the worker to think through what his relationship to each child means to the child. Even though one child may seek and be given a good deal more attention than some of the others, this does not necessarily mean that he is a "pet" or a favorite. Someone once said that if a certain child got extra loving, attention and approval out of *the cottage parent's need* for his response, then indeed he was a "pet," but if it was done out of *the child's need*, then it is on a safe basis. The worker may, in fact, feel quite close to, and positive toward the boy or girl who is having the greatest problems and perhaps being the most wearing and difficult member of the group. The very struggle, particularly when the adult is earnestly trying to help the child, brings them closer together.

The Size of the Group

One of the most important developments in the field of child care is that the groups for whom cottage parents are expected to care have become smaller in size. But there is still a long way to go, for there are even today some groups with as many as twenty or thirty members! So much of the effectiveness of the work of cottage parents, and so much of the child's chances for a satisfactory day-by-day life, growth, and improvement, depend upon the size of the group. The values in group living may be stronger or weaker, depending on the numbers of other children with whom the individual must share the adults who take care of him.

Suppose one were to take the children in any group today and study their case histories, keeping in mind all that they have missed of normal family life and parental care, and then add to this the casework, psychological, and psychiatric diagnoses which are often available, telling what this history means in terms of all that each child needs from the staff, and from the setting. After reading a dozen such stories, the conclusion might well be that no one person could possibly do all of this for more than eight to ten children, possibly even five or six, and do it right. As has been mentioned several times elsewhere, boys and girls coming into residential care today present much more serious difficulties than was the case ten or fifteen years ago.

Each individual needs more time, patience, thought, and skill, and each one drains a good deal more out of the worker. It is not humanly possible for a cottage parent to do all that needs to be done when there are too many in the group. The child care staff member is learning more and more about the need for, and the possibilities of a positive use of the group. But the job becomes frustrating to him when he cannot put his knowledge in practice, because the group is too large.

When we think of it from the point of view of the children, we know that most have suffered from parental deprivation. Each child needs *one-eighth* or more, *not one-twentieth* of the cottage parent's time and attention. Otherwise we are only again placing the child in the position of being deprived of adult care. And the housemother or housefather has to spread himself too thin, has to divide himself among too many youngsters. When the group is large, each member will continually want more concern with himself as an individual than he gets, will clamor for it, and will feel frustrated much of the time because he does not get it. He will always be placed in the position of competing with others as he brings his needs to the attention of the houseparent. Small children in large groups often develop loud, insistent, high voices in their efforts to gain attention for themselves, and the most aggressive (but not necessarily the ones who need it the most) manage to get it. The quiet, withdrawn child may give up, may recede into the background, or be overlooked and left to himself with his problems and conflicts, which only grow worse with lack of attention.

Another point in favor of reasonably small groups is that there is less of an impact both on members of the group and on the cottage parent of extreme and sometimes bizarre behavior, of emotional upheavals and outbursts, of demands, and intensity of feelings. This is wearing enough in a group of eight or ten, and a point of no return is reached when additional children are placed in a group over and above the number which would have been workable for the members in it, as well as tolerable to the group leader. Having a smaller group assumes a willingness to participate with the child in some of the planning and carrying out of activities mentioned in the chapters on play, clothing, and a place for the child's possessions. With a smaller group there is not only more time for the child himself, but also for these things which are such an important part of his world and life. There is time for the houseparent to talk things over with individual children, rather than, as is often the case with too large a group, when he or she finds that communication is carried on in a mass directing of traffic, "Let's all get ready for bed, now," or "Hurry, it's time for school."

It is easier for a new child to be received by a small, rather than a large, group. In the larger group where the members may already be vying with one another for the attention of the cottage parent, the admission of still another child adds to this feeling of competition, and the new one is not likely to receive a warm welcome from the others. Nor is the cottage parent, already distraught by a large group, able to give the new child the extra time and attention he needs during his first days.

The Composition of the Group

Whether or not a child will find a positive climate in his group depends not only on the size of the group, but also on its composition. Most institutions find that the homogeneous arrangement works out best, that is, an all-boy or an all-girl group within an age span of about three or four years.

One housemother spoke of the difficulties which she was having because the age span in her cottage was much too wide. Actually she was required to try to cover two groups, eight smaller girls (seven to twelve) in one dormitory, and eight older girls (thirteen to seventeen) in another wing. There should, of course, have been two housemothers in this cottage instead of only one. The difficulties with which this particular worker was concerned were that the older girls required and insisted on most of her attention, presenting much greater demands on her time and energy than did the younger group. She was well aware of how much the younger ones needed her, but they were always being short-changed, in fact, actually neglected by her, causing her great frustration as she saw all that could and should have been done for them which she was unable to do.

Continuity of Leadership

Whether group living will offer a positive experience depends greatly not only on the quality of the leadership but also on its continuity. Much that might be positive will be diluted, upset, thrown out of gear, or completely lost when there are too-frequent changes in cottage parents. When a good houseparent has been with an agency over a reasonably long period, offering strong leadership, his group may be settled into a good climate and spirit. Individual members will be making progress. The cottage or dormitory might be looked upon with pride and relief by the director, since everything is going along as smoothly as a group ever can. Then should the cottage parent or parents change, there is always an upheaval. If the worker has been well liked and has been able to give the youngsters real security, the group will feel a sense of loss and possibly resentment over his leaving. The group might work out its feelings by making life difficult for the new worker. Then, if this person in turn leaves, the group becomes even more upset and difficult, feeling guilty over behavior which resulted in the new worker's inability to take it and to struggle through, as well as feeling uncomfortable with the sense of power that they were able to bring about the leaving. The very group which may not have offered anyone any particular concern when in the care of an experienced and well-established worker might become a problem group during a series of changes in leadership.

While a change in cottage parents is always difficult for a group as a group and for the individuals within it, and while everything possible should be done to keep turnover in child care staff at a minimum, still there is a small degree of comfort in the fact that, for the children experiencing this change, several other factors remain constant. That is, the place stays the same—the general framework of the agency, the program, activities, meals, and daily life do go on. And other members of the staff who are concerned with the child, the director, the caseworker, other cottage parents, represent continuity.

3. The House

Whether the house where the children live is an old congregate building or a more modern cottage, it can offer much that is positive as the setting in which troubled youth is helped. It may, on the one hand, strike a note of solidity, permanence, color, warmth and comfort, suggesting activities which invite its use, if it has a lived-in look. But, on the other hand, if it is highly waxed and compulsive in its order down to the precise placement of the last stiff chair, then it is as if a forbidding, denying, restricting cold hand were laid upon the child and his natural inclinations.

First Impressions

The child who comes to an agency on a preliminary visit, or the one who is coming to stay, is usually going through a low period in his life. Often he comes into placement after a series of harassing experiences which may have shaken, upset, shocked, and drained him. The past has not been good. Now he is confronted with another setting, a Children's Home. And no matter if it goes by the name of School, or is gaily called "Sunny Farms" or "Happy Acres," the child is likely to take a dim view of what this new place will be like. In fact, the association which most people make—adult or child—who have had no experience with specific modern institutions, is one of dull, cold, drab surroundings, rather than one of color and warmth. And so, it is most important that the lobby of the administration building which the newcomer first enters, or the entrance to the cottage, or department, or wing where his dormitory is, be one which extends a welcome and gives some cheer through the colors on the wall, the pictures, plants, furnishings, and tangible evidences that young people live here, as well as some toys and children's magazines to occupy the child who has to wait for a few moments. The adult knows how his spirits may be lifted or lowered by the decor, and the date and condition of the magazines in the office of the doctor or dentist. And here in the lobby, plaques listing donors' names who have given generously to the institution sometimes fifty or a hundred years ago, or pictures of long-past presidents of the agency do not speak to children of hope for a cheerful experience. The promise of a new start and anticipation of days to come cannot be suggested when one is stared down upon by pictures of elderly Victorian ladies and gentlemen, admirable as they may have been in their time.

The Dormitory

Those agencies which are fortunate enough today to be building cottages to replace congregate buildings are able to incorporate into their plans good principles of child care and psychological knowledge. One of the greatest needs is to move away from the dormitory plan and to provide arrangements for as few children as possible to sleep in one room. Rooms for one or two work out the best. But many institutions must still operate in cumbersome old buildings and make such adjustments as are possible for their physical structure. This is much more difficult than starting out anew with modern cottages.

One of the first problems which comes up in adapting out-

moded buildings is that of having some degree of individualization within the dormitories. Many have high ceilings, they
may be long and narrow, and are usually anything but cozy.
But in spite of this, some institutions have made effective use
of ready-built units which not only divide a dormitory into
cubicles, but also include in their construction dressers, closet
or locker space, and shelves. One advantage of these structures
is that they can be moved around and various arrangements
tried out. They are available in various colors. Another advantage of those which include dresser, shelf, and locker space
is that a child may keep his clothing and possessions within the
immediate area surrounding his bed. He does not have to go
off to some distant locker room or dressing room. His sleeping, dressing, hair combing, and other personal activities are
confined within an intimate, private, and compact area, a little
enclosure all his own.

Plastic bricks, which admit light but are not transparent,
offer another means of dividing a dormitory. While individual
cubicles do not in any way provide all of the advantages of
single or double sleeping rooms, they do go a long way in
providing some degree of privacy. They help a boy or girl
feel, "This is *my* place."

It is true that dividing a dormitory into cubicles will take up
some space that could be occupied by a few more beds, but this
is perhaps a good thing. Often too many are crowded into a
dormitory with insufficient space for clothing, toys, possessions,
and physical movement. Although there may be adequate
cubic air space, as measured by formal standards (when ceilings
may be high, allowing for plenty of air to breathe), the beds
may be so close together that they do not permit adequate
room for each child to move freely around his own bed. A

youngster gets irritable when there are so many others constantly so close to him. This only results in his wanting to push, kick, and fight with those who are always infringing on his small area.

Dormitories were often planned and placed in the most desirable parts of the building, to catch all the sun and light possible. It's regrettable, in those cases where their use is still restricted to sleeping only, that they cannot be enjoyed for more hours of the day. They might very well double for playrooms, or one end be furnished as a living area, with some comfortable chairs, possibly a davenport or day bed, lamp, book tables, and a radio.

The Bed

We might ask ourselves whether the child is allowed to use his bed as much as he would like. His bed is, after all, *his* bed. So many other things he must of necessity share with the others, and thus his bed has a special personal meaning. Given free rein, he comes back to it again and again during the day, to touch home base, so to speak. The younger child will keep his most treasured, beloved and shabby possessions on top of his bed, and at night, *in* it with him. Some of the live pets will take to sleeping on the beds, too. And why not? The child who is inwardly uncomfortable and lonely can be helped by the presence of his familiar bear or doll, as well as the physical comforts of a good mattress, a pillow, woolly blankets and bedspreads that feel soft to the touch and look warm in color. One still sees, unfortunately, the perfectly made hard bed, with its clean white bedspread, and the unused doll or animal in the dead center of it. This is a sad picture, really, and in no way expresses the child and how he is. Real life isn't this way. A dormitory made up of rows of such beds no longer impresses most visitors in any but a negative way. It is for appearances and it is not for children. But appearances for whose benefit? Why do not all institutions by now have the security, the courage, and freedom, to break this pattern which has brought much criticism to the field?

While still on the subject of the bed, and what it means to the boy or girl, mention should be made also of where it is placed. Sometimes a nice sunny dormitory room is furnished only with two rows of beds and two rows of chairs. The beds are placed a foot or two from the wall, toward the center of the room, in order to facilitate cleaning. There are no toys other than the obviously unused and unloved ones sitting stiffly on the bed. The floors shine with wax, the air is fresh, and the room has a sterile, unlived-in atmosphere. The child does not go to bed here with all of the comfortable preparations which might be made for bedtime. He undresses in a dressing or locker room, leaves his clothing behind him, and approaches the bed as one would a stranger, as it sits out there in space. As we think of what is wrong with this picture, we need to go back again to the fact that most children who come to institutions have moved and moved, and do not feel settled anywhere. They need to settle in order to be helped, to feel that they have a place, an anchor. One way to help the child gain a hold somewhere is ideally to give him a corner where he can have the reassurance of walls on two sides of him to hold him in, protect him, walls that he can touch and know that they are there. Children need to touch to be sure, and the child whose bed is out in space where his hands cannot reach the walls is only given the feeling that he is still adrift. There are, of course, not enough corners to go around, but at least we can give each boy and girl a wall for his bed to touch. Of course the walls will get messy but they can be washed and repainted—necessarily more frequently in a children's Home than in a family home. Often individual houseparents are quite willing to change traditional patterns such as the rigid dormitory described, but may hesitate to break a set way of doing things which has become entrenched throughout the entire building, or they may not be given the "go ahead" by the board and administration to do so.

A Place for the Child's Own Things

One of the most important arrangements to work out, and again, this is harder in a congregate building than in cottages, is a place for each youngster's toys, possessions, odds and ends, collections—the things he has brought with him and those he accumulates as he goes along. In comparison with the average child in his own home, the one in the institution usually has pathetically few possessions which represent a tie with the past and which he would like to keep on into the future. These belongings are, as mentioned in the chapter on "Play," an extension of self and they add to a much needed feeling of self. In this connection there are usually three kinds of frustrations for the child; first, he doesn't have enough room for his things; second, they disappear, or someone else uses or breaks them; and third, the housemother who places too much emphasis on neatness and order urges him to get rid of some of the things which cause a clutter but may be dear to him.

Part of the houseparent's responsibility is not only to provide a reasonably individual place for each child's possessions, but also to protect them, to worry along with the child whose toy disappears, and to help him restore it. It often takes considerable time and patience and a lot of sleuthing to trace down

a lost article, but when the adult does this each time a plaything is appropriated by another child which is not rightfully
his, it is better all around. The one from whom something has
been taken feels that things have been made right again; the one
who did the taking will be stopped before this becomes too
much of a habit. We are placing the youngster in a position of
constant frustration when he can rightfully complain, "You can
never keep anything around here!"

There is less danger of losing things, or of having them taken
when there is a place for them near the bed and within the
immediate living unit rather than when they are in a playroom
in a distant part of the building. It is easier for houseparents to
keep their eyes on each child's possessions when they are in or
near the dormitory and adjacent area. The visitor to a children's institution who has observed boys and girls in their own
homes with their many belongings in evidence is inclined to
wonder and to ask, "But where are all of their things?" The
toys, the cut-outs, games, books, animals, jump ropes, roller
skates, balls, tennis rackets, stacks of comics, and so on and on
that one would expect to see are still all too little in evidence.
This is a real weakness and an unsolved problem in such a number of institutions that it suggests the need for some new
thought and consideration as to how this part of the child's life
might be made more satisfying to him.

It would be good if each child could have: 1) a closet, or,
second choice, a locker for clothing, with perhaps shoe space
below; 2) dresser space, at least two good size drawers; and
3) some sort of a toy shelf, together with a box or chest with a
lock on it. In some cases, two children might share a dresser,
placed between their beds. When we remember that boys and
girls are being prepared to return to a family home eventually,

we want them to do the obvious thing which is to keep their underclothing in dresser drawers. True, the dressers of some will always be in disorder. This adds to supervision time and trouble but we are not seeking for the easiest way for staff to manage, but rather for a way of living that will be useful later on. Another advantage of dressers is that they have mirrors, and youngsters need mirrors and use them a good deal when they have them. They increase recognition of self. As we work toward the goal of helping the child increase his own feelings of self-worth, one way we can do this is by providing a place for his comb and brush, and toilet preparations with which he can enhance himself, and a mirror in which he can admire the effect. Boys and girls like dressers too, to put things on. Connie and Janet lived in a group of adolescent girls. At sixteen and seventeen each had, on the dresser they shared, a picture of herself at age two or three. Each baby had been very much prettied up for the photographs, which were tinted; they looked like plump, placid, loved babies, and these pictures, carefully framed, had great meaning to the two girls. Their placement careers had begun when they were about six. But in their display of these two baby pictures, the girls seemed to be expressing the thought, and to want others to notice, "They did love me once. They dressed me up and had my picture taken; I was once a little child who was loved by her parents." It helps youngsters like these two when the housemother provides a proper setting for such family pictures, and appreciates fully how important this is to them.

A child should not be expected to keep his toys and other articles in the dresser or closet with his clothing. He needs another place for playthings and odds and ends. An orange crate, placed the tall way, makes quite a satisfactory individual toy or book place. It can, without too much trouble, be given a finish with sandpaper followed with a coat of shellac or varnish and lined with wallpaper or painted on the inside. Youngsters like an activity of this sort, particularly if they are making something for themselves, which will be one answer to an almost always present need for more individual space for their things. Boys and girls of almost all ages like and make good use of individual desks, or a desk which two may share. A desk provides additional drawer space; older boys and girls use it for study; and younger ones use the top for various kinds of play, construction activity, drawing, anything which requires a surface area. Often children in institutions have too little surface area, such as tables and desk tops, to work on.

Comfortable Furniture

Everyone likes and needs a soft place to sit at times. We want children who have come into care feeling tense, distraught, restless and on edge to be able gradually to relax and unwind, to a degree at least. Tension can be eased a little by outer comforts. And, as is the case with many of the symptoms which children in groups show, we welcome even a degree of improvement, less tension than when admitted. Comfortable furniture is not a cure but it helps. It suggests and is conducive to relaxation, at least for a few moments here and there. When one sees a restless hyperactive group, it may be observed that perhaps they really have no place to "light." We should welcome the child's desire to lie down for a few moments, to lounge. He may want to use his bed for this and should not be discouraged from doing so. If there is a davenport or day bed in or near the dormitory, it will be in frequent use. Window seats on which a child can sprawl are popular, too. The trend is to include some comfortable pieces of furniture in the dormitory or smaller sleeping rooms. This again helps to pull all of the living processes closer together rather than maintaining them over a wide area, with the youngster having to go to a living room at some distance from his sleeping room to find a comfortable chair.

Bulletin Boards

One of the most popular articles of furnishings for all ages is the individual bulletin board. Bulletin boards can be found in stationery and department stores in attractive bright colors for around three dollars. Most children seem to have a desire to put things up on the wall. When individual bulletin boards are provided, this need is not only met, but the putting-up is confined to the bulletin board rather than all over the walls. They offer a way for the child to express his interests (movie stars and sports figures); his achievements (his own drawings); to show that he has friends (birthday and Christmas cards, valentines and invitations); and that he has a family (snapshots of parents, brothers and sisters). A study of the variety of things which are displayed on the bulletin boards of individuals within a group tells quite a story in itself.

Housekeeping

Children as well as staff respond positively to beauty, color, and comfort throughout the buildings. When efforts are made to provide an aesthetically pleasing background with comfortable but still sturdy practical and usable furnishings, and to introduce variety and interest through the use of pictures, colored curtains, and patterned washable wallpaper in dining rooms and kitchens, this all conveys to the child that the institution staff and board feel he is worthy of such a pleasant setting. He gets the feeling, "If they like to fix this up to look nice for us, then they like us." Such a backgound can be maintained too for youngsters whose previous experiences causes them to be belligerent, hostile, and destructive. There is no need for the setting to look the way they feel. In fact, the appearance of the living unit can go a long way toward making them feel better. Fresh, clean-looking pastel walls raise the spirits, and dull drab colors depress them. Interesting studies have been made of the psychological response to color, and the use of colors which give a lift has been given careful consideration in the decoration of schools, hospitals, offices.

The boy or girl whose own feelings are disorganized is not reassured when his surroundings are in this state also. In fact, to be able to lean for a period on the order and certainty of the physical surroundings may be of help to the youngster with great inner disorder. A framework of order is necessary; children whose own lives have had no dependable pattern or consistency can make good use of it. And the cottage parent needs to have a plan and an organization of the day, of household supplies, of the children's clothing, and play and activities materials. But within this framework of order and good housekeeping there should be allowances for a comfortable clutter. It is quite workable to permit the free use of all of the rooms and at the same time maintain an acceptable standard of housekeeping. And this again brings us to the point that the appearance and orderliness must not be too important; it should not have priority over on-going activities of the group. A good question for a staff member to ask himself or herself is, "Is this for the impression it will make if someone should drop in unexpectedly, or is it for the children?"

Institutions have a good many visitors, sometimes unexpected. A director may reassure a staff that it is not expected that everything must always be in tiptop shape. But still, the individual housemother will worry about what a stranger might think who drops in, such as visitors from other institutions, consultants, parents, social workers, board members. One way that the cottage parent can be relieved of part of the strain of the visitor is for the administration or casework department to let him know well in advance exactly who the person is who is coming, his reason for visiting, and to reassure him that it is not necessary to straighten everything up. The whole practice of visitors going through the institution is one which is an added burden to child care staff personnel, and it is a subject to which the administrative office could give more thought.

One institution took the following step in an effort to solve the problem, to an extent at least. This agency had eight cottages and an administration building. The cottages took turns in receiving visitors, which meant that all visitors in a given week would be taken through Cottage X and Cottage X only. In the administration building they would be told about the work, shown pictures, and all questions would be answered. Thus the staff of each unit had to be ready for visitors only one week in every eight, and could be completely sure the other seven weeks that their unit would not be invaded by anyone not on the staff, and that the administration would respect and protect this privacy. The children need protection from visiting groups and individuals as well. When people phone before visiting, the visit can be directed toward a time when the children are in school so that they can be spared the unnatural experience of a group of strangers going through their living unit, sometimes making them feel like little animals in the zoo. One or two visitors can sometimes be absorbed as guests at a meal, but then again the cottage parent appreciates knowing beforehand who this is, and the children, too, need to be introduced and prepared for the presence of a person previously unknown to them.

To return once more to the actual cleaning and upkeep of a living unit, it is generally accepted now that the cottage parent have some adult help with the heavy cleaning, such as floors, windows, walls, and of course, repair work. The maintenance man who replaces broken windows, light fixtures, door knobs, and looks after the plumbing, needs to be a patient and long-suffering personality, for there are added drains on his time, tools, and resources in a children's Home. It is easier said than done to try to find a person who will go along with this philosophy rather than a type who constantly fights it. But it is important that anything which is broken or has been put out of order be quickly repaired or replaced, and that the house be made whole and strong again.

4. Mealtimes and Snacks

To give food to the child at his regular mealtime as well as between meals, and the ways which this is managed, can offer some of the best opportunities the houseparent has to help the child both physically and emotionally. To be fed well and lovingly is one of the basic needs of all children, and the need is much greater for those who have not had continuous and affectionate care in their own homes.

An infant gets his first feeling of security and well-being from being fed, and from his mother, who feeds him. Crying in anger and with hunger pains causes a baby to become insecure and nervous. When an infant is fed, he not only takes in a certain amount of physical nourishment but he absorbs, as well, a feeling of general contentment when lovingly held during the feeding, together with an oral emotional satisfaction. If he misses this early pleasurable and comforting experience, his need for it may show up strongly later in childhood, during adolescence, and into his adult years. Thus the houseparent may have the older child who sucks his thumb or other objects, the one who wants to eat all the time, chew gum or candy, or smoke.

The lack of loving parental care found in the early histories of most children in institutions usually reveals a general neglect, of which food and feeding may be only one part. Any of the disturbances which are the prelude to the breaking up of a home and the placement of children can cause an emotional void, an empty, unsatisfied feeling. Some youngsters, in trying to take care of this void in their emotional lives try to fill it in another place, their stomachs. A child may have not only an intense need for food, and a desire to eat a good deal at and between meals, but he also fears that there will not be enough. Sometimes he hides food in his clothing, under his pillow, in order to reassure himself. A child may do this when he first comes into care, giving it up only when he has experienced over a period of some time that there is enough for him and for everyone.

When the child meets his new houseparents at the time of his pre-placement visit, or when he comes to stay, it is good to offer him something to eat as a welcoming gesture, cookies and milk, an apple, or a sandwich. Children should feel from the start that this new place has an abundance of food. Plenty of satisfying food goes a long way toward building good institution morale, from the standpoint of both children and staff. Many youngsters whose mothers have worked may have known only catch-as-catch-can meals, the sandwich or sweet roll which they ate standing up in the kitchen, with a glass of milk from the refrigerator. For these youngsters, the simple sure fact of three regular sit-down meals, prepared with thought and care, and with the needs and enthusiasms of children in mind, means a great deal.

No attempt will be made here to discuss meals from a strictly dietary view since many institutions have on their staffs someone trained to plan the balance of foods needed by growing boys and girls. Also, many good books on quantity cooking are available. The discussion which follows might be considered a thinking-through of what might be done to increase

the positive results which can be obtained from food in order
to help along with the feelings of well-being which we all
wish to build up in the children.

When Do the Children Eat?

BREAKFAST. A child's whole outlook on life for the day, his
morning's work in school, are all so much better when he starts
off with a nourishing, tasty, hot breakfast. The institution's
breakfast usually includes milk, cereal, toast (hopefully with
butter *and* jam), fruit, and sometimes eggs. With the wide
choice of appetizing cereals available today it is possible to
serve often the ones that the children particularly like, and to
allow them to have a choice, especially with the variety of
ways that dry cereals are packaged. To top off Cream of Wheat
and Ralston's with brown sugar gives a caramel-like flavor that
enhances these cereals for some. All cooked cereals should be
served very hot with no lumps in them; children hate lumps.
Most youngsters like toast. Like cooked cereal, toast should be
hot and freshly made. One large institution with one hundred
children eating in a big congregate dining room had for many
years prepared its toast the night before, serving it cold for
breakfast. Now there is nothing as discouraging as a piece of
cold toast twelve hours old. A young man who had been in
this institution as a child never forgot this. He happened to see
in a restaurant-supply store a revolving toaster which turned
out many pieces of hot toast per minute, and he purchased it
for the institution. This meant that the children not only could
have their toast hot, but they could enjoy the smell of it as
well as watch and run the remarkable machine that made it.

Many children in institutions wake up feeling depressed,
irritable, and reluctant to face the new day. Sometimes they

are awakened too early and are expected to do certain duties before breakfast. In other words, the time between rising and breakfast is too long. This may suit the routine, but is not desirable for the children. If required to do jobs before breakfast, they will not be able to approach either the idea of work, or the work itself in at all a positive way, and it just becomes a source of further irritability for everyone.

At breakfast, there is a danger that the staff may have a sense of urgency and rush, a need to get the day under way and the children off to school. Houseparents have their morning routine on their minds. The kitchen staff wants the meal served, eaten, and out of the way so that preparations for lunch may be begun. The child may feel that everyone rushes him through. Children have a slower tempo of eating than do adults. Since eating can be such a positive and pleasurable experience, children should be allowed to relish their meals and have some conversation along with them, without feeling that all adults are sitting on the edge of their chairs, impatiently waiting for them to finish.

MID-MORNING LUNCH. Most nursery schools routinely provide fruit juice, milk, and crackers, or something similar in the middle of the morning. When institutional children are at home mornings they, too, enjoy a mid-morning snack. During the periods when they are in school, it has been observed that youngsters who had breakfast at 7:30, or 7:00, or even earlier, liked to pick up something at 8:30 or so to eat at that time, or to take to school with them for recess. The cook might be encouraged to put out a dish of fruit, raw vegetables, sweet rolls, or whatever is available, for the child to help himself to if he wants it at this time, or to fortify himself for a time when he will be hungry later in the morning.

NOON MEAL. The institution which has more small children than adolescents often plans to have its heaviest meal, or dinner, at noon, and a lighter supper at night. Adolescents do better when they have their heavy meal at night, particularly when they are in school all day and may have had a somewhat light school lunch. Whether it be lunch or supper, the lighter meal requires special skill and imagination in its preparation, avoiding the tendency to rely on leftovers. When a basic meal is planned first, say, for example, a nourishing soup, toasted cheese sandwiches, milk, stewed fruit and cookies, then the leftovers can be served too, on the side. This gives children a choice of having part of the extras or not, and we are always looking for openings for them to make their own decisions instead of having too many things arbitrarily decided for them.

AFTER-SCHOOL SNACK. All children seem to be hungry after school, and this is a food time that they particularly look forward to. The school day is over, there is a sense of relaxation, and they are just naturally hungry as they plan a period of usually intense outdoor play before the evening meal. At this time they need something like a big apple, a generous piece of bread with peanut butter or jam, or a fistfull of graham crackers.

THE EVENING MEAL. Dinner, the fullest meal of the day, usually offers the standard meat, potatoes, one or two vegetables or salad, dessert, and beverage. Whether it is served at noon or in the evening, there again is an opportunity to allow the child to make a choice—to say whether he wants a big or a small serving of certain foods. Children need and want different quantities, and the houseparent who is aware of these differences in appetite keeps in mind the big and small eaters. If a child is fond of a certain food, he might be allowed to have more of it than the food that is distasteful to him.

It may seem a little obvious to say that boys and girls should butter their own bread, but one still does find the very brisk housemother here and there, who, in an effort to have everything in readiness for a swift, smoothly running meal, will butter the bread for her table. Even the slow, clumsy, messy child needs to learn to butter his own bread, and what's more, he enjoys it.

THE BEDTIME SNACK. Children's Homes are inclined to serve an early evening meal, often at 5:00 or 5:30. Children usually play actively for a period in the evening and, if hungry, may need a little something to eat before bedtime. Adolescents, who study or have other activities and who do not go to bed until 9:30 or 10:00, usually want an evening snack or something to chew on while studying.

These regular meals, together with the between-meal snacks, convey to the child a sense that he is "given to" often during the day.

The question might be raised here: will not all of these snacks and in-between lunches disrupt a balanced diet? In answer we might say that the need of the child to feel satisfied, well fed, and provided for, that is, his state of emotional well-being, is just as important, or, for the present, more important than the fact that he is given a rigidly controlled balance of food. When the three basic meals with their necessary food values are provided, when the snacks do not precede the meals too closely, and when experience shows that a child can make good use of both meals and snacks, we need not worry about diets and balance.

Food Likes and Dislikes

The cottage parent often feels frustrated when the children pronounce the food "awful," don't like vegetables or salads, want to put ketchup or mustard on everything, and are suspicious of any dish previously unknown to them. Here comes a new, undernourished child who needs to be built up. The cottage parent would like to see him eat all of his vegetables, but the only things he really likes and wants are wieners (with mustard), hamburgers, bread and butter, milk, desserts, and soft drinks. Let's think for a moment why he is being so difficult about food. The hot dogs, etc., may be what he had at home, and children tend to like and want what they are used to. Another child, who has moved again and again, who has been placed and re-placed, has had to make all kinds of food adjustments, according to the cultural patterns, the nationality, and the habits of one foster home or institution after another. Hamburgers and hot dogs are good old dependables, running like a common denominator through all of our culture, to be found at all snack bars and lunch counters. Together with bread and butter and milk, he clings to them like life savers.

Then, too, the harassing experiences of many children have made them suspicious of people, of food, of any number of things. If some sort of a hashy mixture is served, the child becomes skeptical about what is in it, and he meets the problem by quickly saying that he doesn't like it, he doesn't want any of *that*. Children respond better to a plate which shows one at a glance the meal which is on it, and that the foods are known, tried and true. These are potatoes, this is meat, here are carrots, each in its place, not all mixed up. The child doesn't want anyone to fool him, to put anything over on him; he wants to be able to identify his foods. For example, if the menu calls for spaghetti and meat balls, it is better to separate them. The child can then eat them one at a time or he can choose to mix them himself.

There are some foods which most children like and others that are generally unpopular. Children like hamburgers, mashed potatoes and gravy, most meats if well prepared, pork chops very much, also spareribs, spaghetti, milk, and most desserts and fruits. Corn is one of their favorite vegetables, particularly corn-on-the-cob. Among the dislikes are rutabaga, eggplant, squash, and cottage cheese (for some). Tongue they cannot abide. There are enough vegetables and meats and a great enough variety of all foods so that it should not be necessary for a cook to repeat the foods which the largest number of children in any one institution do not like. A good deal of resentment can be stirred up by serving tongue twice a month. Youngsters like things which they can pick up and eat with their fingers (this may be one of the reasons why corn-on-the-cob is so popular).

We must remind ourselves that we expect the new child to make many changes and adjustments to new people, to a different and unique kind of environment, to a group of strange children, and now also to the diet of this particular institution. For some children, all of this together with being expected to use knives and forks more often than has been their habit, and suddenly to have acceptable table manners, is more than they can manage at one time. A young child (and many of those in institutions function at a level below their real age) may have difficulty with the very process of eating. He would rather eat with his fingers than with silver. When a hamburger is served on a plate with potatoes and vegetables, the child would dearly love to pick it up, clap it between two slices of bread, or better still, a bun, and eat it that way, which gives him much more pleasure. The youngster would also like to pick up the chicken leg, the pork chop or sparerib, and chew on the bone; this is natural. We can help along by serving different finger foods, raw carrot sticks (can be on the table regularly once a day), celery, fruit, toast. Rather than a dish of ice cream, the child prefers a cone or cone-like cup to suck and lick.

It is true that the housemother has a responsibility to get the child to eat the dishes which are strange to him but good for him. After he tries a few times, he may overcome his feeling of distrust and actually learn to like a particular vegetable or salad. Most housemothers go along on the theory that each child whom she serves have on his plate a little of everything. If she is wise, she will start with very small servings of those things which he does not know and she will go easy the first months when he is having so many new adjustments to make. Sometimes the sight of one vegetable on his plate which he doesn't like will spoil the entire meal for him. Some boys and girls may be good eaters generally but may have one or two intense food dislikes, and they should then not be forced to eat that particular food. It is good to serve a popular food along with one which is new or less popular. Milk is almost always liked, and milk as a food carries a good deal of significance. It is the baby's first food, and gives him his first security. Milk means Mother, being cared for and loved, being nourished physically and emotionally. It is a familiar food and should be served with every meal. The same might be said for bread.

We sometimes find that children in institutions crave foods or treats that are very sweet (candy, ice cream, soft drinks), sour (apples, oranges, pickles), salty (potato chips and saltine crackers), or highly seasoned (ketchup, pizza pie). This may be due to the fact that some quantity cooking is inclined to assume a bland, montonous taste over a period of time. Thus, boys and girls, and staff members, too, on their days off, seek extremes in food tastes, the unusual.

On the whole, it might be said that many children in institutions would like more meat and eggs (protein), and more fruit, particularly oranges and apples. The latter are craved for their tangy taste, counteracting the above-mentioned blandness, and also due to a possible need of the body for the vitamins and other food elements they provide.

We must keep in mind, too, that food is an obvious thing to gripe about. As we mentioned earlier, many of the youngsters are angry because of their past experiences and the disturbing things that have happened to them. They often cannot direct their anger on its past source without help, so they tend to take it out on the cottage parent, the food, the rules, or whatever is handy at the moment. Or the child may be feeling other frustrations within his group; he may be upset over a change in cottage parents, he may not be getting enough or any casework help with the things that are bothering him. All of this may be making him generally irritable, and the food becomes the target for some of his negative feelings. On the whole, though, in the institutions which have a generally good climate, which are sympathetic and sensitive to the needs of the children, and where the food is good and well served, we find an enthusiasm and gusto for meals and snack time, and there are very likely no more feeding problems than in the general population of children, probably less.

Desserts

The certainty of jam or jelly with the breakfast toast, and the repeated pleasurable anticipation and enjoyment of dessert following the two main meals, means a good deal to the children. They often check to see, "What's for dessert?" before they begin the main part of the meal, having made sure that there will be cake, pudding, fruit, cookies, or something of the sort to look forward to. They like the idea of dessert as well as the fact of dessert. Even if it is a modest dish of stewed fruit with a cookie, or graham crackers stuck together with frosting, it still comes under the heading of dessert. It is, to the child, a treat, a little bonus, something sweet with which to round out his meal. He feels let down if it is not there.

Who Gives Out Food?

It is important for the child to feel that not all food flows from the cooks and from the kitchen, but that it comes from his houseparents as well. This means that the between-meal snacks should, part of the time, at least, be given to the child by the regular or relief cottage parent. This provides a pleasurable experience which balances some of the activities the houseparent is responsible for which are not so popular with the youngsters, to see that the work is done, that clothes and toys are picked up, that baths are taken, the discipline and control. The child may feel that the houseparent expects a lot from him, and he or she surely thinks that there is much about the work that is extremely trying and negative. To make it possible to have pleasurable positive periods with the group in this and in other ways, some supplies and equipment *to do with* are needed. For example, in each department there should be a supply of cookies, crackers, raisins, peanuts, candy, and things like ready-mixes, puddings, Kool-Aid, to use at the houseparent's own discretion, for rewards, or for the child who craves these things. Perhaps a boy or girl needs a little help over a bad moment, or is recovering from a trying experience.

It is good when each group unit can have a family-size toaster, an electric plate, and an inexpensive oven to put on top of it. Children enjoy a simple supper in their own department, cottage, or dormitory, particularly when they have most of their meals in a large congregate dining room. A supper which they prepare together with the cottage parent, even one so simple as cinnamon toast, fruit and milk, can be a real treat. Nowadays we also have the instant desserts, ready-mix cakes and cookies, the ever-popular gelatines, all of which adapt themselves readily to dormitory cooking. The child likes the speed with which something in a box becomes something good to eat. (Remember here the inability of the children to wait very long for an anticipated pleasure.) The cottage parent should also have the equipment to prepare a birthday party, a late Sunday morning breakfast, or some other spontaneous or planned-for special meal. An electric corn popper, together with a supply of unpopped corn and oil, will become a most popular addition to the working equipment of the houseparent. These poppers function miraculously, the smell and sound of popping corn is tantalizing, and an hour of popping and eating corn in an evening can be a soul-satisfying one to the child. A waffle iron serves an equally popular purpose. A boy or girl in a small group may choose to have a waffle supper for a birthday. Or, the waffle iron offers a change when, for example, there are just a few children around on a Sunday evening. Part of the success of the process is for the adult to be able to turn out sufficient waffles, or the toasted cheese sandwiches which can also be made on such an iron, fast enough and long enough to keep up with the demand. This also gives a group a chance to have a hand in the preparation of food. For those children whose basic security is very shaky, there is the reassurance not only of the certainty of an abundance of food, but in addition, there is a special meaning to be able to cook, or bake, to lick pans or stir a mixture, and to actually make things which smell and taste good.

Where Do They Eat?

We try in many ways to work away from mass care of large numbers toward more individualized care and smaller groups. Many institutions which have long been housed in large congregate buildings are in the process of converting to cottage systems. But, surprisingly, even when new cottages are being planned, the question still comes up: would not a central dining room be less expensive, more expedient, more efficient, and thus more desirable? It is true that a central kitchen and dining room are less costly than individual kitchens and dining rooms, but our first concern should be what is best for the children. From the standpoint of their needs there are distinct disadvantages to eating all meals, month after month, with large numbers of other children and adults.

The noise, confusion, distractions, and complications of many children of all ages eating together is not conducive to relaxed meals. The older boys and girls tend to dominate the tone of the dining room, making it disturbing and often confusing for the younger ones. Extreme behavior, a "blow-up" on the part of one child, may upset an entire dining room.

In smaller cottage dining rooms, children tend to be more

relaxed, they eat more slowly, voices are not so strident, and they are not keyed up to such a high pitch. The cottage dining room is just naturally more homey, more comfortable, more like real life. The place where the child eats is part of the setting of his living group, closely related to the other living processes rather than being taken out of it and centralized.

When there are individual kitchens in the various cottages, it is easier to prepare to meet the needs of various age groups. Adolescent boys like and need heavy meals, meat, potatoes, vegetables, and substantial desserts. Adolescent girls, on the other hand, appreciate salads and lighter desserts. Smaller children need a more delicate type of meal, that is, more puddings, cooked cereal, etc. Children up to the age of eleven or so usually accept and enjoy cooked cereal for breakfast. Adolescents in the same dining room, at an age of wanting to be grown-up and of throwing off childish ways and foods, may reject cooked cereal as part of their strivings for sophistication. Their comments and attitude may disturb the contentment of the smaller child with his oatmeal and Cream of Wheat.

There is not only the difference in food needs and quantity, but also in the tempo of eating. The dawdlers are usually found among the children under the age of ten; their eating time is much slower than that of the adolescent. The plan of requiring all children to wait until everyone is finished before leaving a congregate dining room is not a good one. However, it does still happen when members of a staff have not worked out a way to supervise both those who are ready to leave the table and those who are still eating. This means that the adolescents become impatient with the children whose tempo is slower and for whom they have to wait. These younger children are then hurried and not permitted to enjoy their meals at their own speed. In a cottage having individual dining rooms, where there is not such a great distance between the eating area and the living space, the staff member who serves the table can usually keep her eye on those who remain at the table as well as on the children who may be in other parts of the unit.

The Cottage Kitchen

The kitchen that children can go in and out of freely has many advantages. In building new units, or remodeling old ones, there is an opportunity to work toward the inviting kitchen, not a laboratory-like room, not a restaurant, and not a professional chef's paradise. The trend in the American home is to build warm, colorful, comfortable kitchens in which the family can take some of its meals if it chooses. There is more use of color and patterns, of washable wallpaper, curtains, geraniums in the windows, making the kitchen not only a place in which to prepare food, but a room to enjoy. When a cottage or even a congregate building has such a kitchen and when the housemother or cook welcomes the children into it, it will be one of the most popular rooms. The children then have the positive and pleasurable experience of seeing and smelling food being prepared, of anticipating their meals, as well as having the opportunity of lending a hand in their preparation.

One often hears houseparents complain, and rightly so, of the cook or the chef who is touchy and temperamental, and who considers the kitchen and dining room his sole domain. Three meals are served, and that's that! The housemother is made to feel apologetic and fearful about asking for extras for the children or for herself, and the entire kitchen and dining room are out of bounds for children other than at meal times when they are admitted to the dining room, and at dishwashing times when those whose duty it is are allowed in the kitchen to help wash up. It is surprising that it still happens so often today, but it does, and this is an administrative problem to tackle and solve in order that the kitchen may be enjoyed by everyone.

Who Eats with the Children?

It has been fairly well established as good practice that the houseparent eat his meals with the children. In those institutions in which the children have their noon lunches at school, the houseparents have an opportunity to have one meal each day alone, or together with other members of the staff. Also with the trend for more days off-duty per week, the cottage parent has additional breaks from a too-constant program of having most of his meals with the group. It is a good idea, when all of the children eat together in a congregate dining room that the housemother serve a table made up of children of her own group. She knows them best, their eating habits, their likes and dislikes, their ups and downs. But just as important, mealtime can be a warm, pleasurable, giving occasion, when eating together with time for talk, the give-and-take between members of the group, and the group and the cottage parents can add to these relationships.

The Birthday Cake

Any child's birthday is an important day for him and it is particularly significant for the boy or girl in the institution. Usually the experiences he has had before coming into placement have taken away from him a good deal of the feeling that we like to see a child have, of his own worth as a person. We must watch for any and all opportunities where we can begin to give the child the feeling that he is an important person in his own right and that what he thinks, does, and becomes is of real concern to us. The birthday is one chance to do this, perhaps a seemingly small way from the adult point of view, but when we are sensitive to all of the small ways we can do this, we can build up to a total accumulation of positive experiences. A birthday is the child's own day. So many other days, so many other occasions, he has to share with others, Christmas, Thanksgiving, all the holidays. Thus it is good for him that this is *his* cake alone, the kind he chose to have, baked for him by the cook or the housemother, with the right number of candles on it, to be shared with his immediate group or his own brother or sister, as he chooses. Sometimes an institution which has large numbers of children has a birthday cake for all of those whose birthday falls within that week, or for the several who have birthdays on the same day. But when this is the practice, the great possibilities in the individual cake are missed—that the spotlight is for this day, this meal, on the birthday child alone, the lighted candles glow for him, the individual cake and his gifts help him to feel recognized, important, wanted.

5. *Other Routines: Sleep, Baths, Clothes, Work*

As we think through the adjustments which a child is required to make on coming into an institution and living in a group, we see there are food and mealtimes, all the individuals on the staff and what they do, the other children in the group and in the total population, a new school, unaccustomed work duties, and the expectations to come up to a certain standard (in some cases too high) of orderliness and cleanliness. Usually controls are firmer, routines more set, and demands greater than in the boy's or girl's previous experience. Added to the above, the time for going to bed, or rising, and the hours of sleep are still another adjustment to be made, and may stir up quite a few resistances.

Sleep

When, in the preparation for placement, youngsters are told about the institution to which they are going, and are encouraged to ask questions, one which invariably comes up "what time do they have to go to bed there?" Usually their reaction is that the bedtime and rising times are earlier than those they are accustomed to.

But once the child gets used to this, a fairly regular bedtime and rising time do have positive results. Adequate hours of sleep, together with regular meals, and an interest in new activities, some of them out-of-doors, add up to a physical response on the part of many children evidenced by a good weight gain and better color and tone. For some youngsters, too, this may have been the first chance they have had to sleep alone in a bed rather than with one or more perhaps restless brothers or sisters in a crowded room. But getting up and bedtime present some problem areas; many cottage parents worry particularly about the difficulties in getting a group quiet and settled for the night. There are some things to keep in mind which may help to ease, but not necessarily solve, the ups and downs around this part of the day.

People are geared differently when it comes to sleep. Not all individuals require the same amount of sleep, and the one who needs more than the average becomes irritable and tired when he does not get his full quota. The person who can get along on less sleep becomes restless and frustrated when expected to stay in bed too long. Yet we are inclined to fit all of the children, particularly those of grade-school age, into the same dormitory and the same sleeping hours, regardless of their natural inclinations. One of the many advantages of small bedrooms for one or two is that the children who need more sleep can go to bed earlier, and that those who like to sleep until awakened by an adult can do so more easily than is the case in a dormitory where a few early risers may stir up the entire group.

The cottage parent sometimes observes that a group may be irritable, tense, and excited due to fatigue. Group living itself may cause a hyperactive sort of overtiredness particularly in certain age groups, as, for example, small boys around the ages of eight, nine, and ten, who play very actively and with a certain high pitch of excitement. This is aggravated when the group is too large, when the children sleep in dormitories, and when the construction of the building is such that natural sounds and noises are intensified rather than absorbed. Nowadays more thought is being given to the possibilities of sound-absorbing materials, and their use saves a good deal of wear-and-tear on the nerves of everyone. The high ceilings that were so often built in the old institutional buildings meant reverberating sounds, as a result of which there was a good deal of repression of the natural noises of children which can now be taken care of in a mechanical way with materials on ceilings and walls which absorb much of this.

There is also a kind of an institutional fatigue which comes from living in a highly geared group. Some of this comes from emotional tensions, the child's own as well as that of others around him who show extremes in behavior. This is different and more difficult to recover from than the physical weariness stemming from active outdoor play which has given fun and satisfaction. The child who is constantly overstimulated by the group needs a chance to get away from it periodically, to rest. The staff nurse often has this experience with the child who comes to the institution hospital with some not too serious symptoms, perhaps a slight elevation of temperature or a headache. When such a child is in a room alone, with the assurance that the nurse is, and will be, around, he may sleep almost 'round-the-clock. Or, if a housemother keeps one child, say with a slight cold, at home from school and makes him comfortable, he, too, may sleep all day.

We also keep in mind that children in institutions rarely have the chance to waken slowly and naturally as a child does who has had enough undisturbed sleep. The German word for it is *ausgeschlafen*, meaning literally, "slept out." There are usually some who want to get the day going and who waken others. Then there are those who have difficulty settling in the evening and who talk, tell scarey stories, make peculiar noises, or tease and provoke others into keeping them company. The child who is vulnerable is kept awake in the evening, aroused too early in the morning, and thus misses his necessary sleep at both ends.

As to the actual hours of sleep needed, this varies with age groups and may vary during the week-end or vacation periods. Children may be allowed to stay up later on Friday and Saturday evenings, and to sleep later the following mornings. Children between ages of six and thirteen need about ten or eleven hours of sleep; adolescents, eight to ten; but many at this age insist on only eight. It still does happen that children in the younger age groups are put to bed too early (even in quite bright daylight). When this happens and they are in bed longer hours than is necessary, and when left alone and unable to sleep, then it may be that excessive fantasy and masturbation are encouraged. Rising time and bedtime cannot be hard and fast by the clock, nor can they be the same all year 'round. Rather, the cottage parent keeps his ear tuned to the needs of his particular group and the individuals within the group, and varies the hours of sleep and the time of rising and of getting to bed accordingly.

GOING TO BED. Many cottage parents mention the difficulties in getting a group to settle down for the night and the keyed-up atmosphere that is often present at bedtime. If a child is afraid at all, he is afraid at night. It is a form of isolation to get into bed, isolation from the warmth of people, from the excitements of the day and the support of having many others about. The child thinks of anything bad that has happened during the day. Getting to bed may be full of tension and most children resist it.

A houseparent may want the children in bed and quiet for the sake of his own rest and relaxation, particularly after a long and strenuous day. But the more the adult hurries the child (and the more the child feels the adult wants to get rid of him) the more difficult it is to get the youngster to settle down. An important hint here is for the cottage parent to take his time and not keep pushing and hurrying; in other words, to make bedtime a long and leisurely process. The child appreciates a chance to dawdle, and in the course of this dawling he may unwind gradually, and thus getting into bed is not such an abrupt change from activity to quiet. If the adult is relaxed and unhurried, this communicates itself to the child, and his tension is lessened.

One of the most important parts of the houseparent's long day is that period from 3:30 through the children's bedtime. The importance of this last period brings to mind again that it should be preceded by an afternoon rest period for the houseparent, free from interruptions or active duties of any kind, particularly for those who are on 'round-the-clock duty.

For boys and girls of grade-school age, it is helpful when the cottage parent plans a relaxing activity for the period immediately before getting into bed, as for example, reading a story to the group, one which is not too exciting. Finally when the lights are out, the windows raised, and the last child has taken the last trip to the bathroom, it is best if the cottage parent stays nearby, perhaps in a comfortable chair in the hall outside the dormitory or sleeping rooms, not in the spirit of being ready to pounce at the first noise, but rather to give the reassurance of his protective presence. Children do not like to be left alone without an adult. The presence of the house-mother during the period when they are falling asleep gives reassurance during this half hour or so. Quiet radio or record music helps, too.

Almost all younger children and some up to the age of twelve or so like to take one or several favorite animals, cuddle toys, dolls, or perhaps even a gun to bed with them. These toys help to allay bedtime fears and loneliness and should never be discouraged, even when the child goes to bed accompanied by quite a number of his possessions which serve to give him support, companionship, and reassurance.

GETTING UP. Getting up to face another day is hard for many youngsters in institutions. The day does start with such a bang and such a flurry of activity that it is inclined to stir up the resistance and irritability of those who are slow in picking up momentum. One way the cottage parent can make things a little easier is to go around and waken the boys and girls personally with a pat on the shoulder, a good morning greeting, and a few words of encouragement. Fortunately, the loud clanging rising bell is definitely on the way out: it was too impersonal, served only to irritate, jar, and annoy.

Baths and Bathroom

Bathing is usually a pleasurable activity and the bathroom which is part of the group living unit is a popular room. Children like to play in the bathroom, particularly water play, and a group may enjoy bath night and prolong it for most of an evening when allowed to stay in the tubs as long as they want to, to have bathtub toys, and to intersperse the business of getting clean with play.

It is a boon to the cottage parent and makes the use of the bathing facilities more enjoyable to the group when this room is adjacent to the other rooms in the living unit. The staff member is then able to allow the group to use the bathroom freely and to let them fully enjoy bath night when those who are not bathing can be playing in adjacent rooms. This allows the housemother to circulate all over the unit and not necessarily devote herself full time to the process of getting the baths over and out of the way, as may be the case when she has to take the whole group to a bath place at some distance from the living and sleeping parts of her quarters.

In a homogeneous group, the members can run around freely in all stages of dress or undress. The bathroom for a group of adolescent girls will be in almost constant use in the evening, in the interminable hours that girls of this age spend in bathing, washing and setting hair, washing out underthings, and general grooming. They can enjoy this process without always having to be hurried out.

A bathtub is a must, except perhaps in the case of adolescent boys who usually prefer a shower; sometimes a combination of showers and tubs are used. The tub has a number of advantages. It is more relaxing and a child can take a more unhurried soaking kind of a bath which may help the tense youngster to unwind. The tub lends itself to leisurely play with soap-and-water toys, all of which is conducive to a pleasant half hour or so. An elevated tub is helpful to the housemother with small children who need help with the washing of backs, necks, elbows, and saves her from hours of bending way down to the level of the standard bathtub. Children, and girls particularly, relish all of the toilet preparations which enhance the bath, such as bubble bath, colored fancy soaps, water softener, bath oil, hair shampoos, hand lotion, and bath powder. These articles are always enthusiastically received as Christmas and birthday gifts.

For children of grade-school age, two or three baths a week are sufficient as a regular plan, with extras in extremely hot weather and after play in which they get very dirty. For the child who wets or soils, or the one who has very sweaty feet, more frequent baths may be necessary. We try to encourage adolescents gradually to bathe nightly. There is usually more time for leisurely unhurried baths in the evening for all ages than at other times in the day.

It is often a new experience for a child coming to an institution when someone cares that his neck is clean, that he has regular baths, and personally shampoos his head and helps him with his fingernails and toenails. The girls like to have their hair combed, brushed and braided, and ribbons and clips put in. Most children who have not had enough personal attention respond to this help in grooming and gain a new pride and satisfaction in feeling well scrubbed and neatly turned out as they go to school in the morning. The physical contact during the process of bathing and grooming means to the child that the housemother likes and accepts him and that she is willing to help him even with such details as nails. He has probably not had enough of this as a small child, as is the case with many who have suffered maternal deprivation. Perhaps no one before has ever rubbed some good-smelling hand lotion into the chapped hands and wrists of a small boy, and he responds to this attention.

Every housemother knows the scene which begins when one of the group comes wanting a bandage put on a sore. When she takes care of this one, almost all of the others find some sort of a red place or bruise which they also feel needs taking care of. Instead of waiting until the child brings his urgent need for a bandage to her attention, it is good when a housemother has the time, and a small enough group, so that she can take the initiative and offer the children both the personal comforting attention and the evidence of it, of after-bath powder, hand lotion or oil for the youngster with dry, itchy skin. In other words, it is better when the worker goes out to the child with the offer for this attention rather than that the child is always in the position of asking for it. While it is the sore on his knee which gives him a reason to ask for a bit of medication, it is the whole child who is seeking affection, and who is wanting to have something done for himself alone.

The child who wets the bed may need some extra baths, particularly in the morning, so that there is no odor as he goes to school. When a new boy or girl is admitted who wets the bed regularly, it is well if the housemother lets him know as he comes in that she is aware of this, telling him in a matter of fact way that she has prepared his bed with a rubber sheet under the regular sheet to protect his mattress, and explaining to him just how the sheets and pajamas will be taken care of in the morning. Unless he is assured that this is routine procedure, he may be under a good deal of strain, not knowing what to expect by way of staff reaction.

Since bathing and the use of the bathroom can be such a positive experience, we want to make the most of it as with all the other phases of the youngsters' daily care. From the standpoint of the institution, it is well to consider whether everything possible has been done to make the keeping clean process an attractive one. If the water is hard and not inclined to let soap lather easily, what can be done by way of a water softener? If the towels and washcloths have grown drab and gray, can they be replaced by colorful ones? If the same kind of very practical, antiseptic smelling or coarse soap has been used year in and year out, have comparative cost studies been made to see if a variety of more interesting soaps could be substituted? Does the cottage parent have her own supply of some of the toilet extras that make washing, bathing, and shampooing more attractive, plus tooth paste and powder, and an extra supply of toothbrushes and combs, which have a way of getting lost and misplaced?

Bathing time is not all sweetness and light. The very possibilities which water and the setting offer may stir up a group to all kinds of loud excited behavior, horseplay, teasing, climbing, chasing, or enemies getting even with one another; with all of this, the group may give the staff member a pretty rough time. This may be particularly true with a group that has undergone several staff changes and where there is a new cottage parent with whom the group has not settled down, and who has not worked out, as yet, a system or an established pattern around bath night. In the case of adolescent boys it is much better if a male worker, the housefather can supervise the bathing. Big boys do not like to have a housemother, particularly when she is young, coming in and out of their bathroom when it is in use.

Like so many other things, this process of keeping clean may be overemphasized and too much stress placed on it. The repeated wash-up times in the course of a day may be disturbing to the child who had much more casual, even hit-or-miss, care before coming to the institution. Sometimes too much pressure is placed on the children about always washing up before meals and about not getting dirty. Getting dirty is a natural part of childhood which children should be allowed to enjoy and experience. They should feel free to play freely without the restriction of watching, or being watched all the time, to be sure they are clean. Indeed, it may be a youngster with real problems who is afraid of dirt, paint, sand, and anything messy, and it may be a good sign of progress when he begins to relax in this respect.

Clothing

When the cottage parent conveys to the child that his clothing is important, that is, how it is obtained for him, how kept up and organized, then the youngster feels that *he* is important to the houseparent too. Children of almost all ages respond to and like attractive and suitable clothing. This is one of the most tangible ways an institution has of building up feelings of self-worth. Clothing similar to that worn by other children in the community is of particularly great importance to the child because there is a special meaning to the boy or girl in having the same fashions in clothing as that worn by his peers who are not living in the institution. The youngster is already concerned about living away from his parents and in this setting, and the wrong kind of clothing which may, in a real or imaginary way, label him as being an institution child, builds up in him great resistances and frustrations, and feelings of being unfairly dealt with. While attractive and plentiful clothing is needed by boys and girls living securely in their own homes with the daily support and example of parents, it is all the more needed by those in the institution who make use of the build-up and support of attractive clothing because they do not have these other strengths to help along. It sometimes becomes difficult for the institution to keep up with adolescents who attend community schools and who pick up the swings in styles there. One year the boys must have blue jeans, the next year it suddenly becomes khakis. But most institutions have made tremendous strides, recognizing the importance of appropriate clothing to children as they are being given a fresh start and as an attempt is made in all areas of care to increase the youngster's feeling of self-respect and self-worth.

Adolescent girls respond not only to attractive outer clothing, just the right kinds of sweaters, blouses, skirts and shoes, but to new underthings as well. Adolescent girls who come into group care sometimes do not value themselves very highly as persons, as individuals, and neither do they think well of themselves as girls. Some even deny their femininity. This may happen after a girl has had a poor relationship with, or a weak image of, her mother and thus has not had a mother with whom she could identify and after whom she could pattern. The housemother of a group of girls wants the girls to accept and enjoy their femininity; she respects them *as* girls, and helps along with their feelings of well being by making possible pretty clothing which they like.

The clothing which the child brings with him when he is admitted may not be particularly appropriate, or perhaps it is not in good condition. However, it is important to accept and make a place for both the clothing and the toys which the child brings. They represent a tie with the past, with his home and former life. They may have a very special significance because they were provided by the parent. The child will be sensitive to the attitude of his new housemother towards his very own things, particularly because this child-houseparent relationship is a very new one at this moment. In any case, the adult must be careful not to show feelings of criticism of the child's personal belongings, of the girl's hair-do, but to accept the child as he is, with his things, as they are. The housemother will find that even when a boy or girl has outgrown the clothing he originally brought with him from home, he may still want to keep it, and he should not be put under any pressure to discard it or give it to another and smaller child. It may not be in active use, it does take up space, but it has a place in his life.

When the clothing which the child brings with him is supplemented by the institutions' own supplies, and the youngster is taken shopping in order to outfit him, the housemother keeps in mind the need for three sets of clothing: for active play, for school, and for "best." It is a good plan when, as the child is fitted out, all of his things be marked at once with his name or initials. From the standpoint of the housemother, this is necessary in order to keep straight the clothing of members of an entire group; to the child it means that these are his own things. This is another way to make his care as personal and as individual as possible. For the youngster who has already lost so much, it means that he is able to say, "This is *mine;* it has my name on it." This sets him up a little and increases the feelings of self. The marking should include pajamas, underwear, rubbers, and galoshes.

Today institutions usually supply clothing needs by combining individual with quantity shopping. It is possible to purchase at wholesale prices, and to have on hand in a storeroom, such articles of clothing as various sizes and colors of socks, underwear, pajamas, blue jeans, bathrobes, tee shirts, and regular shirts. The housemother may draw on these things as she outfits a child originally if this has not been done before he is admitted, and to fill in as clothing is worn out. Ideally, of course, and to the extent possible, it is good for the child to be taken to a store so that all of his new outer clothing can be tried on and fitted to him, and so he has a choice in the selection. Going to a shoe store each time new shoes are needed, to be individually fitted, is of the utmost importance. All children seem to like new shoes, and this occasion should be arranged to give them all the pleasure that there is in it. It means a good deal to an adolescent girl to be taken to the high school shop in a department store, where there are fitting rooms, and to have care taken so that she can have a properly fitted brassière and girdle. Not to be overlooked either in their importance as articles of clothing, as they help along with feelings of well being, are the warm bathrobes, housecoats, and bedroom slippers. The advent of nylon and other drip-dry clothing means that there is a saving on drying and ironing costs.

Along with the recognition of the meaning to the child of good clothing goes the efforts toward providing an adequate place to keep it. The boy or girl who has sufficient dresser space and a place to hang up clothes is inclined to take better care of his or her things, than is the one who lives where it is too crowded, or where there is too much sharing of space expected. In place of the traditional ugly metal locker of the past, the new and remodeled institutions are using regular or built-in wooden closets which provide more room and make a better appearance. Most effective and colorful ways of dividing a dormitory are available today with equipment which includes dresser and closet space.

There are problems, of course, regarding clothing, as there are problems in connection with all of the phases of care. The child who is scattered and disorganized in his emotions may reflect this in the disorder of his dresser drawers, his locker, and in the fact that his socks are always lost, his sweater is left out on the playground, his shoe laces are untied, and his rubbers disappear. In keeping his clothing organized he may need more-than-the-average help and patience as some other youngster may in another part of the living process. Then there is the child who, as a symptom of his anger or frustration, may tear or cut his clothing. Another may be so enamoured with his feeling of being well dressed (and having no idea of laundry costs) that he may put on a nice clean shirt every day (his own or someone else's).

Almost any institution receives donation clothing, and like the donated toys, this may be more of a problem than help. Donated clothing should not be used to supply the basic clothing needs of a boy or girl but rather should be used as a filler-in. For example, a donation of boy's blue jeans can be used to supplement the regular stock. We cannot really help a child if we clothe him in hand-me-downs. As is the case with toys, clothing which is donated and which is unsuitable may be sent to an appropriate agency, such as the Goodwill Industries.

Work

Boys and girls are usually expected to perform certain duties, first in connection with their own beds and belongings, such as making their beds, keeping dressers and lockers in order, picking up clothing, and washing out socks or other clothing. In addition, most institutions give the child a job which in some way helps along with the work of the cottage, wing, or department. These latter duties may include cleaning, helping the cook, washing or wiping dishes, running errands, or helping with repairs and maintenance work. In the past, the orphanage-type institution was often criticized for expecting the children to do all of the work. Children were, on the outside, pitied as drudges; they had little time left for play, and, indeed, unfair and extreme demands were made upon them. Nowadays much of this has been bettered. Part of the household work is dispensed with by modern equipment, such as dishwashers, mechanical floor cleaners and waxers, and it is an accepted practice that the child care staff needs adult help in keeping the buildings clean. There has been a healthy degree of relaxation, too, in regard to the pattern of extreme order, highly polished floors, and the rigid housekeeping standards of the past, and this in turn has relieved some of the pressure on the children to help maintain this kind of housekeeping.

When the complaint is made today that the boys and girls have no enthusiasm for work duties, we remind ourselves again that the youngsters who are in institutions more often than not did not want to come in the first place. They may meet a work assignment with the attitude, "Why should I? Everybody has gypped me—nobody has done anything for me—why should I work for somebody else?" Adolescents tend to have these feelings more intensively than younger children, yet, at the same time, we expect more of a work contribution from the boy or girl of adolescent age. We must remember, too, that institutions in these times have many youngsters of preadolescent age, which is a time of great physical growth and psychological change. This growth and change, together with the struggles to understand and make an adjustment to the circumstances surrounding his placement, use up a good deal of the youngster's energies. He *is* often tired, and lacking in the momentum needed to tackle a piece of work with any enthusiasm. He will respond better to work requirements in a setting where he has a positive relationship with the cottage parents, and where he has begun to identify with the agency. If a child is fighting everyone and everything all of the time, then he may use his assigned job as just another means of resisting and fighting back. With the broom handle he pokes holes in the rather soft, sound-absorbing materials on the ceiling; he drops and breaks too many dishes; he puts five times too much detergent in the dishwater, making a tremendous foam; and he gets lost frequently, disappearing from the job completely. Even in a happy family, children resist duties. They like to be given to, to have things done for them. And in a family home, a mother may be willing to make the bed for a child who would be expected to make his own in a group.

One thing which is likely to happen in an institution is that the boys are expected to do too many domestic kinds of jobs, and that not enough really masculine duties can be found for them. This may account for some basically healthy resistances. In spite of all of this, we do have to, realistically, expect the children to take part in the work. In a group which has a good climate, the individual may participate willingly because everybody does it. And then too, in the group, as the members make their beds and pick up after breakfast, there are many opportunities to intersperse a little piece of play in along with the work, to visit and chatter with others, with the cottage parent giving a hand here or there, for example, to the child who is just learning to make his own bed. There are some youngsters who enjoy certain jobs and responsibilities and who gain a feeling of satisfaction and pride in doing something well and getting approval for it.

The following points may be helpful in building up a feeling of acceptance of the required jobs:

1. The caseworker who prepares the child for admission can explain beforehand that everyone has a job to do, and in some detail, what these jobs might be. It is then possible for the child to ask questions, to express doubts, and to get used to the idea gradually, rather than to have the job come upon him suddenly and unxepectedly when he is confronted by the cottage parent with a work assignment.

2. Start him in during his first weeks with easier jobs, something he already knows how to do, that he can finish quickly and with a feeling of success. Sometimes when there is resistance, it is because the child does not know how to do the work, and is afraid of making a mistake, and thus being ridiculed by the others, whom he imagines can do it better.

3. As often as possible, assign a job that he may not mind so much as some others. For example, the child who loves to eat may like to help the cook. A boy who has a good relationship with the maintenance man may work willingly with him.

4. Change jobs often; once a week is a good plan, since one week is long enough on a particular job, and a week may seem to be very long to a child. However, here again one needs to make an exception in the case of the boy or girl who gets a particular satisfaction out of doing a certain task, and who wants to continue with it. Tom, for example, came into a boys' group at the age of thirteen, with the feeling that he was a complete failure at almost everything, school, sports, friends, and family. He was, however, good with his hands, and he made his best staff relationship with the maintenance man, following him around and wanting to help. After some months he was allowed to operate the power lawn mower (one with a seat that he rode on and steered with a wheel), and this gave him a feeling of great importance, of being useful, and able to manage and control this piece of machinery. This became

Tom's special job, one that he loved, and it would have been unfortunate to take it away from him.

5. In any group there are usually a certain number of tasks and a given number of individuals. One way to arrange the assignments is to make out a work-list each week, rotating jobs among members of the group. If there were nine girls, then one girl might be asked to wipe dishes for a week, twice daily, but only every ninth week. With such a list posted on the group bulletin board, the jobs may be more easily accepted as something that takes place routinely, and does not become the basis for a personal argument on the part of a girl. Even with such a list there should always be chances to talk it over, and to have adjustments made.

6. Boys and girls need the break of a day off from work duties, just as a staff member does. This is particularly necessary to keep in mind for the child who rarely has a chance to go away from the institution on week-ends or at other times. Sometimes one department, such as the kitchen, finding a willing helper, hangs on to him too long, imposing on him. The cottage parent watches that such a child is not held too long in any one department.

7. The jobs which are required of the children should have some value and meaning to them later, rather than work which is of benefit only to the institution. For example, being expected repeatedly to wax huge expanses of floor is of more importance to the institution than to the youth whose duty this is. On the other hand, there is real point in a teen-age girl learning to wash out her own nylons and to iron a cotton blouse. Most of the girls will later be on their own, and it is well for them to get into the habit of laundering personal things routinely.

8. Boys and girls accept duties in better spirit if the staff member works *with* them, rather than that they do it *for* the adult. A spirit of "we will all do this together," with the adult rolling up his sleeves too, brings better results than if he only directs and supervises. Children should not be expected to do any work which they do not see the staff doing, too.

9. It is well for an institution staff to figure out how much time is required of children daily in connection with their work duties, and whether this time infringes on the necessary three to four hours of play time, which is needed for the boy or girl of grade-school age. Many institutions say that the child's job averages about a half hour a day, with perhaps more time on Saturday mornings when there is a general clean-up, and this seems reasonable.

10. Our work attitudes in life are important. Many boys and girls living in residential care will later have to be completely self-reliant and self-supporting, when there are no families to fall back on. But a good attitude is built up in a good climate where the work assignments are reasonable and thoughtfully planned. We do not want an adolescent girl to have had such an overdose of housework that she forever afterwards has a distaste for it. A job well planned, on the other hand, may make a boy or girl feel needed and important. Through it, he can experience success. But in any case, we always have to remember that the amount and kind of work that can be expected of a child depends on his emotional stability and how well things are going with him in general at the time.

6. The Importance of Play

The boy or girl who comes to the institution has usually had more of life's negative experiences than its positive ones. We want to change this pattern, and play is one of the best ways we have to give children positive hours of fun and satisfaction. The natural impulse to play, to make or build something, to draw and paint, to learn to ride a bicycle, swim, play ball, jump rope, to make believe, and to do these things with someone runs like a thread through the growing years of most children. It is a wonderful thing, this ability of the child to play hard and give himself intently to the planned or spontaneous play interspersed throughout the day. When youngsters play together, it is a pleasure to see their enjoyment of the activity and to know that what they are doing is enhanced by the companionship, the give-and-take, and the stimulation of playing with others. The child's request for an adult to play with him sometimes, and the opportunities this gives—is it fully enough appreciated and used to the best extent possible by natural parents and houseparents?

The institution receives many children who have been so absorbed in their own anxieties and troubles that they did not feel like playing; others may not have had enough toys or room, inside the home or outside, for active play. For them the setting of the group, the space in and around the building, the toys and equipment, together with leadership and program, have much to offer.

Play and recreation cannot be departmentalized as to place, equipment, or personnel. The fact that there is a designated playroom does not necessarily mean that the child will play there when he is in the house. He likes to play wherever he is at the moment. Two boys making their adjacent beds do quite a bit of playful skirmishing around in the process. Four girls wiping dishes together fancy themselves a quartet and engage in harmony singing. A group in the bathroom washing, bathing, and brushing teeth can think of all kinds of play, acceptable or not, that has to do with water, soap, foam, wet wash cloths, and one another. Nor will play be confined to the periods spent with the recreation or group worker.

The institution which has a group worker, a recreation leader, or both is indeed fortunate, but such workers cannot take all of the responsibility for the play life of the child. And so, in this chapter we are going to keep in mind the many hours of play when the boy or girl is in his own living group and when the houseparent is responsible for him. The area of play can be one of the more positive parts of the cottage parents' job. Given plenty of toys, materials, and equipment, many disciplinary problems can be prevented which might otherwise develop when a group has too many empty hours.

As we keep in mind some of the characteristics of children in placement, and the symptoms of their emotional upset, we will consider how the activities program can be of help with the child's treatment and be beneficial to him. While the points which follow mention some of the therapeutic values in play, it should be emphasized that each child selects those things which appeal to him, and then proceeds at his own pace and tempo.

1. Play releases tension. Children in institutions are more tense and keyed up than are most children in their own homes with whom things are going well. Some of this tension is due to inner problems; part of the keyed-up state may be caused also by the stimulation of always living in a group. In any case, the tension needs various kinds of outlets, and play is one of the most acceptable. Think of the steam that is let off when a group plays together in a pool for an hour or two, and the further relaxing effects when bodies are exposed to sun and air. A housemother in an agency giving temporary care to forty children spoke of the added tension which one found in these boys and girls, all of whom had come into care quite abruptly without time for preparation, usually right out of a family or foster home crisis. The fact that this was a receiving home meant that the children were continually coming and going, and that groups had no chance to settle down to any kind of group structure or entity. Thus these children were even more tense than those in other types of residences. This housemother mentioned the value of the wide halls, in active play, in chasing, all of which gave relief to physical tensions. It is a positive factor that most institutions have more room, both inside their buildings and on the grounds, than most other kinds of dwellings, and children need this added space.

2. Play is an acceptable way to release hostility. Because of a child's feelings of anger, resentment, and hostility, we find him being sarcastic, derisive, critical, and using extremely insulting language. His negative feelings may be directed toward staff, his peers, or the world in general. A cottage parent may observe, "He's fighting everybody and everything." We can help him by providing an acceptable vent for some of these feelings (which have to come out one way or another) through activities and equipment. A punching bag is good here—even when one was installed in a residence for adolescent girls, it was given enthusiastic use. A rubberized figure, such as a clown, which when inflated is about the size of an eight-year-old boy, and when struck always resumes an upright position, serves a real purpose for younger children. Boxing with boxing gloves, under supervision, offers another outlet. Boys and girls given large sheets of paper and plenty of paint (out of jars, not boxes) or finger paints, may make pictures or masses of color which reveal extremely violent and angry feelings.*

Dart games, snowball fights, the gun games that small boys play intensely, all help to release aggression. A small girl playing with dolls and a doll house may dump the baby out of its carriage or happily drown him; because it's play, she has no need to feel guilty. Pounding nails or chipping wood when carving are good activities in this connection. A group of boys was given large chunks of clay which, with the help of the leader they were to prepare for modeling. Part of the preparation of clay is to throw it on a board in order to get rid of air pockets. With great glee and much release of feeling, the boys threw the clay on the board with force and abandon, over and over; in fact, the group had more enjoyment in the preparation than from the later modeling.

3. Through play, the child is relieved of some of his anxiety. As he sits and daydreams, or wanders aimlessly around, the child is absorbed in himself, his past, his parents. The child in his own home with dependable parents takes them for granted and doesn't think much about them. They are always there, to be counted on. Being so sure, with never any cause to worry about them or his way of living, this boy or girl can give him-

* R. Hartley, L. K. Frank, and R. M. Goldenson, *Understanding Children's Play* (New York, Columbia University Press, 1952).

self wholeheartedly to school, play, his hobbies and interests. This is as it should be. But children in institutions have "so much on their minds" that they are apt to turn inward too much of the time. With the variety of things to do and things to do with, as well as easily available playmates, a youngster can usually be drawn into an activity suitable to him, by a skillful staff member. Through play, he may begin to find some relief from his anxiety and self-absorption. His periods of being able to lose himself in activity may be fleeting at first but they tend to increase in length as his adjustment improves.

4. Through play, a child can act out some of his past experiences and relive the past. In this way he may work through some of the things which have been bothering him. Anyone observing a group of small girls knows how they get organized for a bit of play by assigning roles: "You must be the mother, I must be the little girl, and Nancy must be the big sister who gets married." And then quite a revealing bit of the past may unfold; the staff member can learn a good deal by observing. In an institution receiving children from an entire state, a group of boys and girls was observed playing "sheriff" and evicting a family from its home. As children work out a situation in this way, they get it out of their systems in part at least, and thus get some mastery of it and control over it. The psychiatrist who is treating a child, the caseworker, and the group therapist all use play as a special technique with definite purpose and direction. When we speak of it in relation to the houseparent, we mean those situations which spring up spontaneously as children organize their own play.

5. Carefully selected toys and equipment give a child a feeling of immediate response and success. Remembering that the new girl or boy often has limited patience or stick-to-itiveness,

little confidence in himself, and perhaps even the impulse to destroy as "no good" anything he tries to make, we choose a certain group of toys which do not require much skill to manipulate, but that do respond and give something in return for some small effort, for example, the Viewmaster and the slides to go with it, kaleidescopes, and the variety of wheel and wind-up toys for the floor, such as the fire engine which responds with motion, noise (the bell), and light (a red one flashing off and on). Even if some of these things may seem too young for the child who becomes absorbed in them, we keep in mind the fact that many of the children function on an emotional level that is younger than their chronological age. Roller skates do not require a great deal of skill and most boys and girls like to skate. Jacks, balls, marbles, tops, and this seasonal type of plaything comes within this group also. Some children, in their previous living situations, may not have been able to enjoy or did not have these toys at the age when they were right for them, so now they go back and catch up, so to say, before they are ready to pick up again and move forward at their actual age level.

6. Play helps the child develop a feeling of self-confidence. When we see a boy or girl who has learned to swim, climb a tree or roller skate, he usually calls out to the adult who passes, "Watch me, look at me!" His pride, his wanting to show off, his mastery of a new accomplishment or acceptable achievement through his own efforts also say, *"I'm good at this!"* He wants to call attention to himself and to have the adult respond with recognition, praise, and approval. For some youngsters we have to build up this feeling that they are skillful as a result of their own accomplishments in much more modest ways than mentioned above. These are the children whose muscular

coordination may not be good, who have not had a chance to test themselves out at baseball, on ice skates, or with a bicycle. Such a child may draw a picture which the housemother puts up on the bulletin board, calling attention to something the child has done, no matter how simple or crude. And members of the staff, knowing how important this is, give him recognition and encouragement for his efforts which perhaps he has not had before.

A housemother described what it meant to Beverly, thirteen, to learn to knit, as follows. "Beverly learned to knit here. She is a girl who is afraid of everything. In the beginning she was very emphatic that she could not use her hands, saying that whatever she did with her hands—housework, cooking, sewing —wasn't well done. We bought colorful yarn for her to knit a scarf. This is good practice, not difficult, and not too long a job. She learned to knit very quickly but for a long time she refused to turn the needle to start a new row. I would have to do this for her. Beverly had an enormous urge to show important people what she could do, so she had to show her teacher and her friends that she could knit. The teacher was nice enough to start a new row for her. For quite a while she took the knitting to school with her, and every night she put it under her pillow. She is very proud of her scarf and will soon finish a second one." It is out of these seemingly small satisfactions and little accomplishments that a feeling of self-esteem begins to emerge and develop. The cottage parent watches all the time for these opportunities to give recognition, in order to build up in the child a feeling of adequacy and to off-set his own tendencies toward helplessness.

7. The child's feelings of self-worth are increased as he acquires toys and possessions. When those things which belong to

a child are his alone, and when he has a place to keep them where they are safe, he gains a feeling of importance and self. When we observe a boy or girl in his own home, even a modest one, we see how he acquires, collects, hangs onto, and cherishes his toys and the strange objects which may mean something to him alone. The first cuddle toys of the baby are needed and clung to, sometimes up through the age of five, or six, even later. Usually among them is a special one which is sought out in times of stress. Not only are there the playthings, but also the special collections. The adolescent girl still keeps dolls and animals on her bed, even through college. More sophisticated teen-agers now collect records, and among their more cherished equipment are record players and radios, portable preferably. A boy may have equipment for hobbies or making aeroplanes, chemical sets, or stamp collections. Many a child up to the age of twelve or so, who may have a good assortment of possessions, also often has a stack of comic books which somehow he likes to collect, keep, or exchange with others. All of these things give a child a sense of ownership and of possession. They are a part of him and a part of his world. They are, in a way, an extension of himself. Using the word selfish in an un-critical way, we might say that children are naturally selfish in the sense that they want to have and they want to keep.

In contrast to the child in his own home, the youngster who comes to the institution usually has a pathetically small collection of possessions. He does not have the year-in-and-year-out accumulation or the toys of his earlier years, which represent continuity. With all of the moves most of the children have had, they have not been able to keep or to accumulate. They have already lost parents, home, old neighborhood, school, playmates, and somewhere along the line, too, they have lost the possessions which might have added to their weakened feelings of self. Such a child who has had so much taken away from him may snatch at whatever he sees, another child's things, group possessions. He is destructive—"I can't have anything for very long anyway, so why take care of anything?" Here is where the staff has to begin to build up "from scratch," to help the child acquire some possessions of his own, to provide a place for them, to see that they are protected, and to begin to help him to develop a sense of mine and thine.

Some may argue that perhaps too much is made of helping the child acquire things, that we place too much emphasis on material possessions nowadays, particularly in the United States. In general it is true that there is great striving to accumulate material possessions, but, by and large, children's institutions are lacking in rather than overemphasizing this aspect, especially in relation to play equipment, toys, materials, and personal belongings.

8. Play provides definite physical benefits. From the point of view of physical growth, play builds up a child's muscular tone and coordination. Hours of play in water, sun, snow, and out in the air are conducive to a good kind of tiredness and a feeling of physical well-being. Children who suffer from inner tensions are often also "tied in knots" physically. We speak of a drawn, tight look. Play can help a child to unwind and relax physically. Many an adolescent boy adds twenty pounds or more to his weight during a year in an institution. If together with the quantities of good food he becomes interested in an activity which produces hard muscles, his ego expands not only because of his accomplishments but also because of his increased size and muscular development.

9. Play offers adventure. Just as the meals in an institution may seem to be too bland and unexciting, causing the child to crave very sweet, sour, or salty things to eat, so also, life may at times seem tame and dull to him. This is particularly true of the child who has lived a life of many changes and experiences, which while traumatic, may have held a degree of adventure for him which he now misses. Many youngsters who have grown up in crowded cities, surrounded by noise, traffic, close neighbors, lights, and excitement, find the country institutions in which they are so often placed pretty dull in contrast. One cannot learn to understand and love the country overnight. When a group of such boys and girls is taken to an amusement park and given a choice of rides, it has been observed that some cannot get their fill of the roller coaster, the caterpillar, or some apparatus that takes them to great heights, stops for a moment and lets them swing in suspense, makes sharp dips at a terrific speed, yanks them about, and finally turns them upside down (and sometimes their stomachs inside out). But it must be clear at the outset that not all children want this kind of an outlet which has a promise of danger to it. The staff member needs to watch for the child who would be frightened and to assure him that he does not need to participate. But we never know this until an activity has been offered and the children's reactions observed.

Sue was a dainty, very feminine, delicate looking girl of eleven. During the winter season a new Sue emerged. In the course of an evening of tobogganing, when the choice was offered of the large or small toboggan, the high, steep slope or the beginners' hill, the most daring front place or the safe middle of the toboggan, Sue chose the largest, the steepest hill, and the most dangerous place, the front, and over and over she tore, with part of her group, down a slope appropriately called "Devil's Hill." The housemother observing her was surprised, not realizing that Sue had all this energy and desire for such a rough-and-tumble sport behind a facade of delicacy. The housemother wondered, too, as she watched the boys and girls together as they flew down and climbed up for several hours, what would they have done with all this pent-up energy and drive if they had not had this and similar outlets? And, furthermore, she thought, there would be no trouble with the group falling asleep *this* night!

10. Play stimulates individual initiative. Before coming into the group, the child may have been dependent on his own resources for free time activity, without much parental or other adult guidance and companionship. Perhaps he lost himself for longer periods of time than are desirable in the passive pastime of TV, just watching. Or, if his own world was lonesome and empty he may have become too dependent on comic books as an escape from an unhappy reality in the more exciting world of the characters and their adventures which are to be found in comic books. In the group into which he enters, something new and stimulating may happen, exciting to his imagination and challenging to his latent abilities. There are toys to play with, stuff to make things from, someone to show you how, and others to do these things with you. The youngster becomes more of a doer instead of a watcher. He may, given raw materials and a creative atmosphere, use his ability or a new-found skill to an extent never before experienced.

11. Through play the attention span may be lengthened Mentioned elsewhere are the symptoms of distractibility, the inability of the child to finish things he started, his flitting from one thing to another, and his lack of patience. Teachers particularly make the complaints: "He doesn't have his mind on his work; he never seems to listen; he can't stick to anything." With a range of activities offered in the group, the child is exposed to a variety of things to do, some one of which may catch his attention, and even absorb him—if only for a short time at first. There is the woodwork shop, the crafts, sports, a pool, ice rink, hill for sliding, sand box, foxhole, materials for drawing, painting, carving. The child has the chance to sample all of them. When an activity "catches hold" of him, and when there is a staff member who gives encouragement, praises him for his efforts, and participates with him in what he is doing, this enhances the activity and encourages him to stick to it. It may be the first time he has had such group and adult companionship in relation to play or construction. He may find something to latch on to that he enjoys doing; he also likes the recognition and approval he gets for his efforts, no matter how small. If we can give him this in one area of his daily life, and if these periods of interest continue and expand, then there is the possibility that there will be a carry-over to some of the less popular activities, such as school and work.

12. Relationships with adults are strengthened through play. If a housemother were to place out on a table a couple of dozen hard boiled eggs, jars of dye, wax pencils, and other equipment for coloring Easter eggs, and if her girls or boys found her at this table as they drifted in from school, the chances are that she would have no trouble stirring up the interest of most of the members of the group who would want to color eggs too. The same would be true if she prepared beforehand and set out the materials for Christmas, Halloween, or Valentine's Day decorations. To prepare for such an activity takes time, materials, and a certain amount of know-how, all of which we would like to see the houseparent have. Children like not only to do things of this kind, but to do them *with* someone. It gives the cottage parent and the group members a pleasurable period of time together; something positive happens. It is important that the staff member stay with the group for some periods of such activity, give individual interest and attention to it, and that she or he not be drawn away to tend to other things. The housemother is responsible for some periods that the children are not enthusiastic about—making beds, picking up clothes, jobs, and discipline. She has to have a balance of pleasurable periods of time; these help to strengthen relationships and this carries over and may make other times easier.

One of the things to watch for here, and this point keeps cropping up again and again, is that the benefits of these projects of the houseparent are greater when the group numbers ten or less. When a group is too large, then we may only add to the child's frustrations and impatience. Others get in his way, he can't get at the materials, he hasn't enough eggs, he is jostled, no one has time to help him.

We could add to the list of ways in which play helps in the total treatment of the child, in addition to being play for the fun of it. The question might well be rasied as to whether these values are taken seriously enough. A cottage parent may make, and repeat, the mistake of interrupting a bit of play in order to send a child on an errand, to go out of doors, pick up his clothes, or wash up for supper. Too often the play is broken into by an adult at the wrong moment. A housemother was observed taking a small group of visitors through a cottage. Half way up the stairs three girls were intently playing a game of jacks on the landing. (Dr. Bettelheim speaks of children's liking for playing in in-between places.) * The visitors were willing and able to walk around the jacks group but the house-mother rather briskly said to the children, "Now run on and go into the basement to play jacks," thus breaking into the game quite unnecessarily.

Playthings should not be acquired on a hit-or-miss, catch-as-catch-can basis, with a deluge at Christmas time, and drought the rest of the year, but rather on a plan of feeding into each department or cottage the articles that the group and the individuals need. In the spring girls of a certain age group play jump rope, jacks, and roller skates; both boys and girls like to fiy kites; boys, to play marbles. Has the institution planned for this season? Just as there are standards for feeding children and certain things which should be included in the diet, so are there also certain necessary ingredients in the play program and equipment, but as yet they usually have not been so carefully planned or budgeted for.

Another aspect of play which might be re-examined is competitive sports. When emphasis is placed on "making the team" or a league of the teams of neighboring institutions, with silver cups and a great to-do over the winning group and the most successful players, always some boys and girls are left out. Some do not have the skill to compete in sports and games. Since youngsters who come to institutions have already experienced failure in their life situations, our whole emphasis should be on building up opportunities for success, even in the most modest ways. The recreation program should not set up situations where a number of children will fail or cannot take part,

* Dr. Bruno Bettelheim, *Love Is Not Enough* (Glencove, Ill., Free Press, 1951)

and this is inevitable where there are highly organized competitive sports.

However, there can be sports without the element of competition. Given an ice pond and a pair of skates to fit everyone, then each child who wants to skate can do so at his own tempo. One value in the group is that usually the largest number in the group are learners, and the beginner does not feel self-conscious. Or, if there is a pool and a swim instructor for the summer, then each youngster should be allowed to take the initiative according to his own readiness. With baseball, everyone should have a chance to participate who wants to play, no matter how clumsy his efforts, and for the sake of playing today, not for the sake of building up a winning team. We have to remember here again that the child who has been placed is troubled by various inner pressures. Whenever possible, we try to ease up on rather than add to pressures from the outside. Competition and striving for goals too high for him, trying and failing, these things add outer pressures.

One of the complaints sometimes heard in relation to the use of play equipment is that it is no use to have phonograph records, record players, or bicycles, because the children break them, do not take care of them, and nothing lasts. Part of the problem of destruction goes back to the total climate of the institution. The degree of destruction is less when the general climate is positive, when the child lives a fairly satisfactory life within his group, and has a pretty good relationship with the group leader. Destruction is also greater when there is not enough equipment and too few toys in relation to the number of children, and when these things come sporadically rather than in a regular way which can be counted on and anticipated.

If a bicycle were to be made available for the first time to a group of fifteen boys, and without supervision, this bike would, of course, not last very long. Each one would be fighting for his turn to ride and would be frustrated and angry because no one individual could have it as much of the time as he wanted it. The "what's-the-use" attitude of impatience and a feeling of futility that develops is taken out on the bicycle. When a new piece of equipment is introduced for the first time, it is best to do this under close staff supervision. A new record player may need to be kept in the houseparent's room, brought out for limited periods, and operated under control and supervision. Then all of the children have the satisfaction of its use, there is no criticism of the group when something is broken. But gradually, if group climate is good and the group leader's relationship to the group is positive, the chances are that it can be left out more and more of the time. It is better to have this close staff control when it is needed than to turn a new piece of equipment over to a group and then later criticize them for never taking care of anything. A good test of the climate and program of an institution is how *little* must be kept under lock and key. At the same time we must face the fact that when a whole group uses a piece of equipment, the wear-and-tear will be greater than it would be if it belonged to children in the average family home. Also, we recognize that with youngsters whose behavior is at times impulsive, combined with anger, frustration and hopelessness, these feelings may be taken out on a toy, a record, or a piece of china in the dining room; and that this will require a certain amount of replacement. But just because of wear-and-tear, there should not be a waste-land as far as toys and playthings are concerned, nor a withholding punishing attitude toward the group for a condition or attitude which may stem back to climate, leadership and method, and a general lack of equipment.

We have mentioned various activities and the values which children may gain from them while having fun for the sake of fun at the same time. This leads to the subject of equipment, toys, materials, space, from the standpoint of the institution as a whole as well as the tools which the cottage parents need to work with. This will be discussed in the chapter which now follows.

7. Play Equipment

Any houseparent is heartened and encouraged when he or she sees supplies and play materials added in a purposeful way at all times of the year. This is a tangible evidence that the director, the recreation or group worker, or the supervisor of cottage life are doing all they can to give the child care worker the wherewithal to help provide enough interesting things for the children to do. The following suggestions for needed equipment have generally been divided according to outside and inside activities, although some equipment may be used both out-of-doors and in the house.

Outside Equipment

PLAYGROUND APPARATUS. On the grounds of many institutions can be found certain standard tried-and-true pieces of playground apparatus—swings, jungle gyms, and other things to be climbed on, crawled through, or swung on, together with exercise bars of various kinds. Sturdy playground-type swings are good in that they do not require much skill, they give a quick response, and children use the swings for five or ten minutes here and there for a kind of aimless, soothing interlude. The jungle gym is valuable, too, because most children like to climb, to try their muscles, and this is an approved thing to climb on. Tents and sleeping bags are good to have on hand, either for overnight trips or for boys who need a change and who welcome the chance to sleep out on the institution grounds in the summer.

Then there are the vehicles which, when available, are always given vigorous use—the little red wagon, scooters, tricycles, sleds, toboggans, bicycles. Bicycles are indeed a headache to supervise and to keep in repair, but they are among the most popular pieces of equipment. Bicycle riding, like swimming, appeals to most children. When the child whose attention span may be short and scattered in connection with many other activities has a bicycle fairly suitable to his size, and if he can use it undisturbed by others, then, with perhaps just a little adult encouragement, he will doggedly stick to his efforts to learn to ride, for hours on end.

On the grounds there is usually space for baseball, football, and a basket ball standard. A tennis court can, in colder climates double for a winter ice skating rink if originally constructed with later flooding in mind. A sand box, which will need a fresh supply of sand twice a year, or better still, just a good sized pile of sand, is used a good deal by children under twelve. The sand *box* is usually associated with smaller children, and its frame limits activity. A *pile* of sand larger than that which can be contained in the average box will serve more individuals and will be acceptable to a somewhat older age group. This play requires no special skill. Given a few sand toys or small cars and trucks, youngsters will play in sand for quite long periods. Children like, and need, to play with natural materials—sand, water, snow, mud, and piles of leaves in the fall. The sand pile fills part of this need.

While the swings, the ball field, the jungle gym suggest or define the activity, it is well also when a part of the grounds invites imaginative play. An unkempt area which lends itself to digging, building, dragging things around, is desirable. Good-sized sawed-up logs or tree trunks will have vigorous use for building forts and such. They stimulate initiative. The institution which has well-groomed lawns needs also an area of wilderness, a disheveled-looking place. It still happens too often that the inside of the buildings themselves are too neat, clean, and orderly for a child to be completely comfortable, and he needs a place out back where he can play, build, and dig around in the dirt and not have to pick up and put everything away when he is finished.

SWIMMING POOLS. The director of a school for adolescent girls once said that she would not be able to get through the summer if it were not for the outdoor pool and the swim instructor employed for the season. The periods in the pool, often as many as three daily in very hot weather, were the high light of each day; life centered around the pool all summer. Another director said that while the pool of his institution cost so-and-so many thousand dollars, it was worth a million in its benefits to the one hundred boys and girls in residence. What the pool offered could not be replaced by any other activity. Lucky indeed is the agency that has a pool. First, most children like to play in water. Second, a pool appeals to the young boys and girls as well as to those of adolescent age. They make up all sorts of water play and do not tire of this activity all summer. Third, the institution which has a pool usually offers swimming lessons. To learn to swim gives a youngster a real sense of achievement and does a good deal to build up his ego. But the other values of this activity are probably just as important as the ultimate goal of learning to swim and to dive. Play in water is unwinding and relaxing. After a swim, children like to play around in the sun; sun and air on the body also make for relaxation and feelings of physical well being. Given water to play in, children show no lack of imagination or initiative, and the activity is usually terminated by the adult before the children are ready to stop.

For the agency for whom a standard pool is not possible, there are to be had, nowadays, portable pools of various materials as well as the sturdy and almost indestructable army and navy surplus pools. These portable pools appeal to children up to the ages of eleven and twelve, and while they are usually not deep enough for swimming, they do lend themselves to many hours of water play. In this connection, Sister Elizabeth Marie, the Director of St. Domenico's Children's Home in St. Louis, writes, "We are serving twenty-four boys and girls between the ages of six and fourteen. Until last summer we used the army water tank, eleven feet in diameter and three feet in depth. The army pool lasted two and a half years, and could still be repaired if necessary. Most of the damage was caused by the elements of nature rather than hostile attacks on the children's part. We found it so valuable that last summer we expanded the facilities on our own grounds to include a much larger pool. Water play is necessary and enjoyable for every child but is of greater importance to the rehabilitation of the disturbed child. I do know that much hostility can be expressed and worked out through the harmless medium of the give and take of a water gun fight."

GARDENS. A chance to have a garden plot of his own, to plant something, water it and watch it grow, is usually a completely new experience, particularly to the city child. Gardening will not appeal to all children; no one activity does. But certain boys and girls get a real satisfaction and feeling of accomplishment from gardening (as well as reassurance in regard to food), and a chance to have a plot should be offered when possible, together with the interest of a staff member who shows the child how. The boy or girl who is not adept at nor interested in types of outdoor play that require skill and coordination may experience success in the more gentle activity of planting and tending a garden. He needs help in selecting rather sure-success seeds, things that grow quickly and produce some tangible products, such as radishes, pumpkins, gourds, and the hardier flowers, zinnias, for example. The course of a garden will never run smoothly. The child who plants his first seeds often pulls up the radishes daily to see how they are coming along. He is inclined to water profusely for the first weeks to try to speed things up, and to let the plot run to weeds and drought toward the end of the summer. It is not usually a show place; in fact, it will probably look somewhat unkempt. Another child who wants to "get even" with the owner of the plot may pull out his plants or take his pumpkins. But even with all of this, one goes ahead and should not be defeated. Staff supervision and interest keep these casualties down to some extent. As in the case of clay modeling or finger painting, it's the process, the doing, that counts and not necessarily the finished product. Boys and girls also like to have plants in their rooms, something that is alive and growing, and needs care.

Inside Equipment

In discussing the materials which follow, it will be with the thought that these things are a part of each cottage or dormitory unit, so that each group will have certain equipment and supplies to work with at all times.

DRAWING, PAINTING, COLORING MATERIALS. Here we make the materials available and let the children proceed on their own, remembering always that often they do not draw or paint for the end product of a picture or scene, but rather to express how they feel. For this reason it is well to have a generous supply of big sheets of inexpensive newsprint which is around at all times for free use. Pencils, and a good-sized box of large thick crayons give the child the wherewithal to proceed on his own. A school-type easel is good, also, but this and the paints and brushes to go with it may need to be kept in a closet and used at specific times under supervision, at least at first. The easel has a section for holding jars of paint made simply by mixing powdered paint with water, providing a large and comparatively inexpensive quantity. Large brushes and big sheets of paper are better than small brushes, and jars of paint are better than paint boxes, all allowing for more freedom and imagination. This activity is better than the coloring book or the paint book which require the child to fit his activity to a ready-made pattern and to stay within lines. Children left to themselves are often better artists than those who design coloring books. For some children who may be too fearful or inhibited to use paint and paper freely, and who are accustomed to coloring books and dependent on lines, coloring books may be needed until such children feel more free to go ahead independently. The things they draw and paint, whether it is just an arrangement of color on a page, or something more conventional, can often be made a part of the decoration of the cottage or the offices. Many institutions in need of color and interests on the walls, particularly in the many long hallways, overlook the opportunity of using some of the productions of the children here. Mounted on appropriate mats, framed or not, paintings of young people set off a modern colorful note of interest and also emphasize that this is a place where children live.

BLACKBOARDS. The blackboard is popular as a permanent part of any cottage or wing, especially for boys and girls under twelve. A place can usually be found along a hall where a blackboard can be built in or solidly fastened on the wall. They are available in attractive green. When a group has such a blackboard, the chances are that there will be one or two children using it much of the time.

CLAY. A material that appeals to children because of its malleability, because it can be used to express fantasy and to release aggression, and because it is messy, is clay. Children prefer the kind of clay that hardens so they can keep what they have made of it. They like to work with a sizable amount. The kind of clay that stays soft and can be used over and over, which comes in small quantities, does not offer the same satisfactions as standard clay, nor does it serve the same purpose. It is possible for the houseparent who is not able to get regular clay to make a synthetic substitute mixture of equal amounts of flour and salt, with enough water added to make it workable. This does not have the same values as clay, but it does offer a certain attraction, in its workability, and in that it hardens after a child has shaped something from it.

CONSTRUCTION KITS. Planes and boats which come in do-it-yourself boxes appeal to most boys. A little more challenging and of interest to the boy of adolescent age are the "Customizing Kits" of small model cars which they assemble and customize. It is well when the houseparents of boys' groups have a supply and a variety of these kits from the very simple, to the more complicated models, for use the year 'round. Conducive to interest in this activity is a good-sized work table to spread out on, where glue, varnish, and paint can be used freely. It works out best, too, when this does not have to be cleaned up after each spurt of activity, but can be left out so that the boys can keep returning to it. Often the frustration for a group of boys intent on such a project is that they are expected to "clean up and put away" too often, and it is better if an activity of this kind can be on-going, rather than planned for certain set periods. When such a table is near enough to the living part of the unit, the cottage parent can keep an eye on it.

TABLE GAMES. Two or three card tables, to be set up and taken down as needed for games, are useful additions to any group. It is helpful to the houseparent to have a supply of games for such times as the group or part of it is in the mood for this kind of play. Included would be regular playing cards, as well as special card games, checkers, chess, Chinese checkers, Monopoly, Scrabble, dominoes, puzzles, and other table games of which there is a wide selection for boys and girls of all interests and ages. For the institution which does not have a recreation or group worker, it is a good idea to seek the advice of a worker specially trained in recreation who can give advice on the best and most interesting of this group of games.

SPOOL KNITTING, KNITTING, SEWING, LANYARD BRAIDING, WEAVING. Some children like a bit of pick-up work, and spool knitting is simple and has a quieting appeal. Little girls often seem to be interested in learning to knit, and are more intent on the process than the finished product which may show signs of a good deal of struggle and wear-and-tear. Some older girls like to knit, particularly if it is something for themselves. Boys often learn lanyard braiding at camp, using pyrolace, and they enjoy the process as well as the result. Weaving on small simple looms is interesting too. The kind of sewing card sometimes offered, where a child is required to follow certain numbers, may be nerve-wracking to some. We have to remember that with all of these things a boy or girl should never be pushed into a handicraft activity. Some people like to do things with their hands; others do not. What may be soothing pick-up work for one youngster may have just the opposite effect on another and do nothing more than put another pressure on him. The point is to offer a wide enough choice of activities and not necessarily expect each child in the group to be enthusiastic about doing all of them.

WOODWORK, TIN AND LEATHER WORK. In a boys' cottage, even where there are boys as young as six years, it is a good idea to have a good solid work bench, the kind you find in school manual training workshops. Here, if a cottage father were to collect orange crates, some odds and ends of blocks of lumber, together with nails, hammers and a few other simple tools, he would have no trouble attracting the interest of a group of boys. They more than welcome (and need) a chance to pound nails and to build something. A block of wood on top of which he nails a smaller block becomes, to a small boy, a perfectly satisfactory boat. The institution which has a well-established workshop for older boys (adolescent girls like this, too, and are often not given the chance) should not forget the younger ones and their strong urge to pound things together or to take things apart. Every housemother of a boys' group has complained at one time or another that the boys took apart, or took part of, the radio, record player, TV set, clock, or vacuum cleaner. A good way of preventing this is to give a group an acceptable and planned activity along these very lines. Board members are usually willing to bring in old alarm clocks, radio parts, springs, doorknobs, and other parts and pieces of discarded household equipment. When such a collection is put in a big box and turned over to a group with the O.K. to take things apart some more, this affords great satisfaction, and at the same time saves wear-and-tear in the department. If there is no one on the staff who has the time, interest, or necessary simple patterns for things that children can make out of wood, it is often possible to find in the community a manual training teacher who can give some hours on Saturday, after school, or during holiday periods or early evening. Such a teacher might need some orientation to the aims of the work which is different from the purpose of the woodwork class in an average school. We do not expect the child in the institution to make a fine, finished piece of woodwork. Rather, he should be given a chance to make something unpretentious for himself, a little boat, a wooden box (with a lock) for his belongings, a bedside table (orange crate up-ended) or a small shelf for the wall near his bed. There are books available on things to make from scrap and orange-crate lumber. Since an institution often expects too many feminine kinds of household work duties of a boy, there need to be activities to counteract this. Work with wood, tin, or leather offer more of a masculine-type craft. Institutions usually have plenty of surplus tin cans and a number of things can be made from them which are attractive to boys, including the camping-out stove. Tin is good, too, because of the vigorous pounding that is needed to beat it into the desired shapes. Leather companies are usually willing to donate scraps of leather, and a crafts teacher supplies the patterns and leadership. Here too, children usually like to make things for themselves—a purse, comb holder, fancy belt. In some institutions, children have regular weekly periods in a crafts room working under the direction of an arts and crafts leader. For the child who is really interested in this type of activity, this period of time is not enough and may leave him frustrated, wanting more. The value of having a good deal of this activity centered within his own group is that he can work at it for as long a period and whenever he wants to.

DOLLS AND DOLL HOUSES. Doll houses for small girls should be practical, for active everyday use, and not elaborate. A housemother together with her group can very well make their own doll houses out of orange crates, furnished with ten cent store furniture and small family dolls. Girls also like regular size dolls, cradles, buggies, plenty of clothes in which to dress and undress dolls, as well as bathing equipment. These things, together with miniature versions of such household wares as brooms, vacuum cleaners, dustpans, cupboards, dishes and cooking utensils, small stove, and a low table provide the setting and articles with which little girls re-live past home experiences and make up present ones. Because they are not living in a family-type house, they need to play at housekeeping and to play out family life situations.

DRESS-UP AND COSTUMES. One of the favorite kinds of play of little girls is dress-up. They like high heels, and fancy dresses such as those which once were worn by bridesmaids, anything which suggests fairy princesses, or being grown up. The housemother who has a girls' group needs a chest of such dress-up clothes as part of her regular equipment. Given a rainy afternoon, a group of girls with a dress-up chest will keep themselves busy for hours, acting out all kinds of fantasy and make-believe.

When boys and girls have access to costume chests, as well as materials such as burlap, old sheeting, and masks out of which they can make their own costumes, a great deal can be learned by observing how the child outfits himself; how he imagines himself as being; how he would like to be. Boys like to dress up, too, particularly for such occasions as Halloween, in the cowboy and Indian suits that are always welcome as Christmas and birthday gifts. Boys of all ages seem to like fancy or "character" hats and caps, and some boys collect these. One sees baseball caps, Indian headdresses, cowboy hats, fireman and space helmets, and army and navy headgear. Many a housemother has seen her boys amble around the cottage or dormitory in the evening, perhaps wearing only pajama bottoms, with a fancy hat or cap of some kind on their heads.

GUNS. A gun and holster seems to be part of the equipment which goes along with a small boy nowadays, and most boys like to play gun games. If they do not have toy guns, they use sticks or carve something resembling a gun from wood. Sometimes a boy asks for a gun because he has not become acquainted with the wide variety of other toys. Moreover, to wear a highly decorated gun in an oversized holster gives him tremendous prestige with his peers. It may also bolster feelings of bravery and at least give an outer show of toughness to the boy who is not so brave underneath. Playing with guns is not going to make gangsters out of a group any more than reading comics excessively would be directly responsible for making a delinquent. The reasons for delinquency and gangsterism lie much deeper than that. We may as well go along with small boys having guns. They play "good guys" against "bad guys," and the "good guys" may win. And we must remind ourselves here again, that these boys are bothered by feelings of hostility, and that by means of games with guns they play out some of their hostile impulses. Merely denying them guns will not eliminate the hostility.

The thing for the institution staff to concern itself with is that a wide enough range of activities and equipment is offered so that the boys also take part in other kinds of play. The real concern is not that boys will play with guns but that they may play with them to excess if left too much on their own without adequate equipment and leadership to organize other kinds of play.

RECORD PLAYERS AND RECORDS. A sturdy record player, together with story as well as musical records is welcome in any group. The story-telling or story-singing records for younger children offer many possibilities of which much wider use could be made.

BOOKS AND MAGAZINES. The field of juvenile literature is one with which child welfare workers of all kinds might well become better acquainted. Those who work with children are too often familiar only with the classics because they themselves have read them. But there is today a wide and rich selection of the more modern books for boys and girls in good editions and with the best in illustrations. Many of these more recent books are of interest to youngsters of adolescent age for whom there is less apt to be good reading material in institutions than there is for younger children.

Institutions do have books. The problems are that, first, these are not the books that would have been selected if the staff had had the chance to make the selection with the help of a good children's librarian. Second, the books on hand may have been brought in by individuals who wanted to get rid of them rather than because they are right for the various age groups, chosen with their needs and interests in mind. Third, the books are not often enough a part of the unit where the child lives; they are not easily accessible.

Just as we feed seasonal toys into a group, so should the institution have a plan for continually adding good editions of well-selected books to the shelves of the various groups. It would be well if all the adults who work with children had a firsthand knowledge of the best in juvenile literature. The cottage parent who reads to the group at bedtime obtains some of this through reading aloud. Sometimes the youngster who has not had the patience or attention to read books himself becomes interested as he is read to. Often when the staff member begins to read a book aloud, interest may be aroused to the extent that the child wishes to finish it on his own, or is anxious to have the reader go on with it the next night. When a houseparent reads a story aloud at bedtime the children enjoy not only the story but the fact that they are also having the full and undivided attention of the adult. It is sometimes said that the setting of the group is not conducive to children reading by themselves. It is true that there are always others for the child to play actively with. It is true too that most children in institutions are at an age where they prefer active play rather than settling down quietly with a good book. However, when books are available, readily accessible, and when there is adult interest and a willingness to read to the group, one does find the reading pump being primed, and enough of the children learning to enjoy books, and books being read to an extent which makes it worth giving our best thought and care to this subject.

The local library is able to provide lists of good magazines for youth of all ages, and children like to look forward to the monthly coming of their own group magazines. The idea of subscribing to a magazine for a group appeals to organizations who would like to make a contribution and may need some direction as to the needs and wishes of the agency. In addition to the magazines which are subscribed for, for a group, individual boys and girls like very much a gift of a magazine subscription. Such a magazine may be along the lines of special interests—a sports, airplane, or hobby periodical; a monthly Mickey Mouse, Donald Duck or Classic Comics; *Jack-Jill*, *American Boy* or *American Girl*. A child likes to receive mail and the regularity of his own magazine arriving on a definite day each month or week not only provides something to look forward to, but the certainty that it will come has great value, too.

Keeping the Equipment in the Living Unit

One of the factors which makes more effective and successful the use of the toys, materials, books, and other equipment mentioned in the preceeding pages is that they be concentrated near the living and sleeping units. When there is a complaint that playthings and materials disappear or are destroyed, one reason may be that they and the places where they are kept are too decentralized. That is, the child may sleep in a dormitory on the second or third floor, be expected to play in a basement playroom, and to use the living room and dining room on the first floor. Most children in institutions come from crowded homes where all of the processes of living were in one compact, and often overlapping, area. Suddenly in a large rambling building, the child's interests, belongings, toys, and those of his group seem to him to be scattered and lost. When a room is restricted to sleeping only, or a hall is nothing more than a bare hall, when all play is supposed to take place in a remote recreation room, this is not conducive to constructive play. A housemother with a group of little boys may often feel frustrated in that her sole contribution seems to be "riding herd," that is, keeping track somehow of a restless, noisy, destructive group who want to chase and smash and make a lot of noise doing it. To offset this, the institution which has the dormitory arrangement might try to establish several play areas in corners of the dormitory or in the halls outside of the large sleeping room, even if it meant that a bed or several of them would have to be removed. There is often much waste bare hall space, which with the addition of play tables, blackboards, shelves for toys, could be utilized for play. For the active group of small boys, the housemother could establish a number of play areas in and around the dormitory where they do most of their living; a box of little cars, trucks, and other wheel toys in one corner; a game on a card table in another corner; planes, boats to be constructed on a big enough table along the hall; a blackboard fastened to the dormitory or hall wall; paper, pencils, crayons on a table elsewhere. This affords a variety of activities, materials, and interest centers to attract a range of interests within the group. It is possible, too, that the group will divide up into twos, threes or fours in the various play areas and will be more inclined to "light" rather than chase. All of this will take place under the houseparent's watchful eye. This is better than when all of the group is expected to be doing the same thing at the same time.

Other Activities

DANCING. Girls respond eagerly to the opportunity to participate in rhythmic or beginning ballet dancing, and again it is important to remember that it is the dancing itself, even on a very simple level, which is important, and not dancing as a preparation for any kind of a show. Some little girls who may be quite clumsy and not too well coordinated, or unable to keep in step or follow a rhythm, might still fancy themselves as being quite good and, in fact, like dancers they have seen on television or in the movies. Their own feeling of pleasure in movement as they are helped with rhythmic dancing is the important thing. There should be no element of competition in the course of the dancing lessons, no feeling that the "ones who do the best" will be in the show or whatever.

Institutions which have teen-age boys and girls often plan occasions where dancing is taught or practiced. Adolescent girls usually teach one another to dance, and as a rule they are more advanced and adept than are the boys. The opportunity should be given them to invite in boys from the other cottages or boys from the community. Sometimes such groups respond to well-directed square dancing, an experienced caller usually knowing how to get individuals to take part and to learn the steps or forms. Whether it is square dancing, rock-'n-roll, or the more traditional ballroom dancing, the teen-age boy and girl parties need the most skillful leadership and management to make the occasion a success. Sometimes an institution which has had weak planning and a resultant poor party gives up too quickly, saying that it is not workable. The results may be better when a committee of the boys' and girls' groups has taken strong part in the planning, together with the staff leaders in charge of the party. Adolescent boys can be their most trying at such a party. They want to dance, but hang back and don't want to. They feel uncomfortable and dash outside, usually finding a ready girl to dash out with; they feel foolish and are overcome with self-consciousness; they act bored but they want to be there. The leaders may wonder if anyone had a good time; usually most of them did and would return for another party (with many doubts and grumblings expressed which might not necessarily express their real feelings). But with skillful leadership such parties can be managed and are worth while.

Boys and girls like, too, the other parties such as those which can be held at Halloween and Valentine's Day, which allow for dress up, or not. Such an occasion may be directed by the group worker, the recreation worker, or a committee of cottage parents, preferably working with representatives of the various cottage groups. Often children have not had, before coming to the institution, chances to take part in such carefully planned parties, where boys and girls enjoy one anothers' companionship and that of members of the staff. For the institutions which are not coeducational, it is most important that boys be invited to girls' residences, and girls, to boys' residences, for parties of dancing, music, games.

DRAMATICS. One activity which has as much appeal to grade-school boys and girls as to adolescents is dramatics. This activity usually requires a special leader. When there is a group worker, he may use dramatics in a purposeful way to help a group or an individual with problems, growth, or development. Or, the group worker may direct the Christmas play which has as its purpose both the spiritual value of the play itself as well as the meaning and importance to the boys and girls playing the various roles, in receiving recognition.

MUSIC LESSONS. There are always some boys and girls within any group with interest and talent who could make good use of music lessons. Dancing lessons, music lessons, swim instructions, all increase poise and self-confidence.

TELEVISION. Most institutions have television, in fact, it is easier to acquire than many of the other kinds of equipment mentioned. No attempt will be made here to discuss all of the pros and cons of television for children other than to mention that it is, or should be, just one part of the complete play and recreation program. One of the negative points often mentioned in connection with television is that the child is wholly an observer; he makes no effort himself; he loses himself in the fantasy and we remember here that the fantasy life of a child in placement may already be rather extreme. Television should not be given too prominent a place or allowed to assume too much importance as is sometimes the case when there are not enough other activities. There is a danger, too, that it may be used merely to keep the children quiet and from underfoot. But television may not be as much of a problem in an institution as it is in some families, for in a group there are always others to play with actively, there is a planned recreation program, and there can be control over the hours of viewing. When a good program of activities is offered to the groups, together with leadership, most youngsters will prefer the activity, particularly if they are enthusiastic about the leader.

At this point the houseparent may be thinking: "How can I do all of this in addition to just taking care of the child? How can *I* be a recreation worker too?" And other readers may be wondering if perhaps too much is not being planned for the children. If the houseparent will go over the points listed here a second time, he will see that he is not expcted to *do* so much more, as it is hoped that he will be given more things to *do with*. In other words, it is hoped that the groups will have additional things to play with and materials to make things from which they can use by themselves with the houseparent keeping an overall eye on the group and on the equipment. Rather than adding to the houseparent's work load, perhaps these suggestions may lighten it.

RECOMMENDED LIST OF SUPPLIES FOR HOUSEPARENT TO HAVE IN OWN SUPPLY CUPBOARD IN COTTAGE OR DEPARTMENT

For Use in Activities; for Birthdays, for the New Child, for the Sick Child; to Keep in Mind Particularly for the 6–15 Year Age Groups

FOR BOYS AND GIRLS

Blackboard (better if attached to wall), chalk (white and colored), erasers

Card tables

Large table to accommodate entire group

Newsprint paper for drawing and painting

Large box of crayons

Watercolor paints—powdered, in jars for mixing

Pencils

Colored construction paper

Scissors—one for each member of group (blunt "school" scissors)

School paste—large jars

Clay

Children's magazines appropriate to group

Dress-up box

Birthday candles

Christmas tree decorations

Crepe paper

Books appropriate to group

Hand puppets

Viewmaster and slides

Card games

Puzzles

Table games

Cut-out and color books

Old magazines for cutting up (board members and volunteer groups willing to donate)

Scrap books to be filled

Postage stamps (board members often willing to save and donate)

Kites to make

Box of colored cloth scraps, felt, yarn, ribbons

Pyrolace for braiding lanyards

Box of wood scraps

Scrap leather (leather companies often willing to donate)

Spool knitting

Weaving looms—small and simple

Record player and recordings, including those especially made for children

Radio

FOR GIRLS, ALSO

Doll house, furniture, small doll-house dolls

Dishes

Cupboard for dishes

Play household equipment—broom, carpet sweeper, washing and ironing toys

Jacks and balls

FOR BOYS, ALSO

Hammer, nails, tool chest equipment

Flash lights

Construction sets, such as Mechano sets

Blocks of scrap lumber

Aeroplane- and boat-kits for construction, glue, paint

Box of small cars, trucks

Marbles

In response to the questions sometimes raised as to whether too much is not being done for the children by way of planning and playthings, it might be said that the children should and will have many periods of time when they are on their own. A child may want time alone just to putter. Many of the materials and much of the equipment mentioned give the child something to do and to play with for those times when he alone, or when the group makes up its own activity. The cottage parent may not need to be a participant, but rather to suggest the activity and make the equipment available. The adult keeps a supervisory eye on the group, if even from a distance. It must be remembered, too, that many of the playthings mentioned are seasonal, and that the needs of not just one group, but the entire range of ages, has been considered. And then we always keep in mind that the child in placement has not had the kind of background conducive to the development of inner resources and initiative as the child in a secure home has had. The average child in an institution needs more suggestion, support, and direction by way of programming, leadership, and equipment to help him approach the time when he develops skills and creative initiative more strongly within himself.

SUGGESTED READING

Parents' Guide to Children's Reading. New York, Pocket Books, 1958.

8. Discipline

The disciplinary problems which confront the cottage parent are often troublesome ones, and this is a subject with which help is frequently sought. But unfortunately here is an area where it is difficult to generalize and to be as helpful as one would like to be. A way that is good in handling one child in his particular group might be harmful to another in a different group.

Perhaps it would be well, first, to think of what is meant by discipline. The word does not mean the same as punishment, even though the two are sometimes used interchangeably. Dr. Irene Josselyn, in her chapter on "Discipline" in *The Happy Child*, tells us that the term is derived from the Latin and means "instruction and training." As used here, it will be in the broad sense that the cottage parent teaches the child and helps him to grow up in the right way; punishment and the management of difficult behavior is just one part of this. Discipline applies to adults, too. A person may be said to work in a disciplined way, that is, there is some plan, purpose, and control in what he does, and a good deal of thought as to why he proceeds in a certain way and not in another.

The cottage parent sometimes questions whether, with the new understanding and approach to the care of youth in groups, with encouragement for self-expression, verbally and otherwise, children today may not be given too much freedom, and whether the institution is growing too permissive. And thus we start out with the principle that the institution should and does set controls. A director must be able to keep things under control in the total setting, and the cottage parent, in the group. Boys and girls need to know that they can be controlled. If a child reaches the point where he "runs" his parent or substitute parent, he becomes fearful and anxious. He worries about the strength of his own impulses. Who is going to protect him when he needs protection?

But there is a difference in our concept of control today and as it was regarded by the old time orphanage. In the past there was often a much too rigid control. Children were expected to obey just for the sake of obedience. They were not encouraged to say what was on their minds and they were fearful of acting out their impulses in any way. This repression was carried out in the extreme order and the rigid appearance of the buildings. The staff would not relax in the regimentation they felt was necessary. They seemed to be convinced that "if we give an inch, they'll take a mile." As a result, children were repressed, and they conformed outwardly to these inflexible barriers. But their feelings inside were often seething.

Nowadays we are trying to teach boys and girls to conform because of strengths they will build up within themselves. This can best be done by an agency that offers control and protection along with other values, such as a good play program, and opportunities for helpful staff relationships. While it is true that children need to know where the limits are and need to be held to them, they also need to be free to practice, to have choices, to make mistakes, and to blow up once in a while. One sees the successful cottage parent combining a firm management with warmth, giving, consistency, and enough relaxation to give individuals in the group freedom for some degree of self-direction and self-expression. Children do not mind a strict cottage parent if he or she has these other qualities. It is sometimes difficult for the cottage parent to accept the degree of freedom possible within the boundaries of a situation where the adult is the final authority. There is still often a certain apprehension of being more permissive in practices such as allowing the free use of the house, or greater individualization within the group.

The Total Climate

In thinking through its problems in connection with ways of handling difficult behavior, the institution is sometimes inclined to consider certain children or groups and to look at it from the point of view of what to do about this boy or this girl or that group. It is well, at the same time, to analyze, "How are we, the staff, doing? Is there some rule, or some practice, or way of handling things that we might think of adapting, or changing? Could this difficult situation have been avoided or handled more effectively in some way?" And so, it is necessary first to go back and look at the whole agency. The cottage parent will have less serious problems within the group if the total climate or morale of the institution is positive. Such a good total climate, in turn, depends on a number of factors: 1) the executive, or director, who is responsible for the leadership of the agency. In speaking of agency morale, Dr. Ner Littner says, "Leadership is a vital necessity—the feeling that one is a member of an organization that is headed by a firm, strong, interested and protective executive"; * 2) the staff and

* Dr. Ner Littner, *Some Traumatic Effects of Separation and Placement* (New York, Child Welfare League of America).

staff spirit, which is built up by means of good working conditions, the feeling that each is a member of a team, that the child care staff member has supervisory help and support, chances to express himself, and to continue to have stimulation in learning on the job (in-service training). A good staff spirit is found more often, too, where there is not too much turnover, where enough members stay to represent continuity. A high rate of staff turnover is not conducive to good climate; the other side of the coin is that where there is good morale, cottage parents are more inclined to stay longer; 3) a strong program of recreation and activities with adequate equipment, materials, and planning so that there is much to capture and hold the interest of the children; 4) a good deal of the total climate depends upon the size of the groups in relation to the number of staff, a point which was discussed in more detail earlier; 5) the physical structure in which the groups are housed. Cottages are more conducive to good climate than the congregate building with large dormitories, central dining room and kitchen; 6) the board of directors and its practices. The board which clings to outmoded traditional ways and insists on carrying on with practices which rightfully belong in the administrative, casework, or other departments, often seriously influences the total climate. For example, the board committee may be unwilling to turn over to the casework department the decisions regarding the intake of new children. Another board may make hard-and-fast orders about practice which is better decided by the staff and executive together. A board may make it possible, in principle and financially, to have groups of eight to ten, rather than twenty or more children. Many boards are, in this period of great change within the institutional field, studying their roles and functions. Their progress in this direction depends to some extent upon the first of the points mentioned above, that is, a strong executive who provides leadership and interpretation to board as well as staff.

Casework and Discipline

Casework services help to carry out the principle that only those children who can be helped in this particular setting are admitted, and that they do not stay beyond the point at which they could also get along in a family home and in a community. The caseworker works with the parents, resulting in the easing up of some of the pressures with which they may have burdened the child. In addition, the worker helps the parents with some of their own problems. The caseworker also has regular conferences with the child care staff member about the life of the child in the group. The cottage parent may use some of this time to tell of troublesome happenings, of upset periods of individuals within the group. "This is what happened; this is how I handled it; do you think I did the right thing?" Such discussions give the cottage parent a chance to test and share his thinking, to get the reaction of another person, to evaluate the actual way difficult behavior was met, to receive suggestions and to relieve any tension there may have been on his part. When there is someone in the position of supervisor of cottage life or supervisor of cottage parents, he may be the one to give help with methods and practices and the handling of specific group incidents. The caseworker will be interested in the same material as it relates to the total treatment plan of the individual boy or girl. The cottage parent who knows that help, direction, and support are always close at hand, together with the sharing of information and responsibility, is not under such a strain as the one who feels he is carrying the greater part of the job all alone a good deal of the time.

Often the houseparent has high hopes that the individual sessions which a boy or girl may have with the caseworker will improve the child's behavior. But the child care staff member is disappointed and sometimes critical when after a period with the caseworker, the youngster is even more difficult than he was before. Or, one hears, "I spend all week getting Joe settled down, and the caseworker manages, in forty-five minutes, to get him all stirred up again!" Let's look for a moment at why this happens.

In the direct casework with the child, an attempt is being made to help him understand, and later to be able to absorb, some of the many confusing things which have happened to him and to his family. This takes time, the process cannot be hurried, and it is hoped that after a period he will feel more settled and at peace with himself. But until this is finally accomplished, the child may go through some rugged periods during his sessions with the caseworker and his behavior in the group may be more difficult.

As the caseworker tries to help the child remember, and to express his own recollections of his previous life and how he feels about it, painful memories are often reawakened. The caseworker, as the child reveals some of the things which may be on his mind, helps him with a bit of interpretation here, clearing up a distortion there, or giving the child a glimpse of insight at another point. By himself, the youngster may have taken the easier way out and built up a fanciful or daydream picture which is much more pleasant for him to think of. To face the reality of the past as well as the present, and some-

times of the plans for the future, can be disturbing and upsetting. But the boy or girl is helped to do so for the sake of
his better adjustment to his situation. The sooner a child can
be helped the better it is, rather than if he carries by himself
all of his feelings and conflicts on into adolescence and adult
years. Sometimes a youngster is able to bring out facts about
his experiences and his reactions to them in a way which he
has never had the courage or the opportunity to do before.
He may go through a good deal of emotional turmoil as he
and the caseworker work together. The process is not easy
for him.

June (Chapter *14*) was more able to face her predicament
than most children are when she said fiercely to her caseworker, "My mother never wanted me, she always wanted
to get rid of me. I'm no good." Harsh facts for a girl to face. It
takes courage to make such an honest, revealing statement,
and it is understandable that a youngster returns to his group
in a state of turmoil sometimes, and needs to have the understanding of his cottage parents, that they be the same, that the
group setting can be solid and dependable to receive him
and give some degree of comfort. He wants and needs to go
back to the place where his group is, to feel that everything is
as usual there, that people will stay calm even if he feels low
in spirits, or temperamental, or like kicking the furniture. It is
reassuring to him to see his housemother engage in some child
care task, unperturbed, a solid, steady person, even when he
is blowing up.

Such questions, accusations, experiences as June brought up
cannot be resolved in just a few casework conferences. It may
take months and months of help before a boy or girl feels more
comfortable. And during these months and this process his

behavior is not better, but often worse. Gradually, when the youngster is freed of some of his tensions and preoccupations, he can give himself with more concentration and interest to school work, play, and activities. Strong as the group program may be, it alone is not enough; most children need, along with this, individual help with their deeper under-lying problems.

Group Factors

If the total climate of the institution is good, each group will be nourished to some extent, that is, each group gets some strengths from the whole. The size of the group has a direct connection with difficult behavior, with the wear-and-tear of its members on the staff, on each other, and on the equipment. A houseparent's problems are greater when there are fifteen or more in the group rather than eight or ten. The worker with too large a number is more harassed and has less patience with the individual. The child is generally more satisfied and settled when he is one of eight to ten. And with a larger group, the houseparent may have to be repressive, more authoritative, to take more short cuts, whereas in the smaller group there is more time and leeway to work things out more slowly and individually.

Certain age groups are easier than others. For example, the seven-to-ten year olds follow staff leadership more easily; they are generally more "groupy" than adolescents. Some housemothers find it easier to take care of boys than girls. Boys are more direct in their behavior, and when they are aggressive or hostile, they come right to the point. Girls are more complicated psychologically, and more adept at finding the vulnerable areas of the feelings of the female staff member and making it difficult for her, either in actions or words. Girls are more apt to be sarcastic and indirect in their manner. Many of them have unhappy experiences with their mothers. Those who have experienced maternal rejection may bring to the housemother some of their anger against women in general. The housemother of a boys' group has the advantage of being a person of the opposite sex. One disadvantage in many institutions is that there are not enough men, not enough father images to balance the number of women on the staff.

Discipline is more difficult when there is a large and rapid turnover in the group. Then members do not have an opportunity to settle into any kind of a group structure. When the houseparent has had the members of the group long enough to establish relationships of some depth and meaning with them, he is able, through the strengths of these relationships, to work out many problems in a positive way. In this connection, Mr. Norman Lourie says, "We need to use discipline as part of a framework that helps people get something from people, and not from rules."

The housemother who has been with a group of adolescent girls for some time, and with whom they feel settled and secure, can insist that they be in at a certain time on movie night, and they will accept this with minimum fuss. The same group with a newer housemother, who is being tried out by them, and who is herself perhaps not too sure, might experience a great to-do when she sets a time for coming in, with accusations that she is not fair. Or, the housemother of a group of boys who excuses from his work one boy who is not ill but who is having a bad day, can have her decision accepted by the others if she has a firm and sound relationship with the group. On the other hand, a less well-established worker might easily be confronted by a critical attitude from the rest of the group, that the one who was excused always gets all the breaks, that he's a favorite, and that they won't do their work either.

The Goals of Discipline

Our goal is not to have obedient conforming children, and a restful milieu for the staff, but rather children who are being helped toward as normal and healthy personalities as each individual can attain. Normal children will be disobedient, belligerent, hostile sometimes, particularly those who have been separated from home and parents. There are many children in institutions who do not want to be there at all. They may not want to be with their parents as the parents are, as much as they wish their parents were the kind of people who wanted and loved their children and would make a home for them. We have boys and girls who tried to get, by difficult aggressive behavior, parental attention which they could not get in any other way, and they cannot change overnight. There is also the overconscientious child who makes an effort to win approval by being very good, and when he acts up later in the group, it may be a sign of progress. Children should have the courage of their convictions, and feel free to stand up for what they think is right and to argue out a point. The cottage parent has to let a good deal of negative behavior go by. There is no need to feel that some disciplinary action must be taken every time a child is insolent or there is an episode of trying behavior, other than perhaps a word of direction. Youngsters should not live under the threat of a possible demerit, deprivation, or black mark whenever they do or say something they shouldn't.

The Individual Approach

The degree or amount of supervision, of control, of insistence on coming up to a certain standard varies and is different for every child. There is the boy whose history shows that he has been fighting everything and everyone. He may have worn out his school, his parents or foster parents, and even had the neighborhood against him. When, in the group, his difficult behavior is controlled, the boy is given a chance to have people respond positively toward him, to receive approval and perhaps to stick to an activity long enough to enjoy it and get some satisfaction himself. The recognition for brief periods of acceptable behavior, together with the success of following through on an activity to a point of even minor achievement, may be a new experience for him. Enough peaceful interludes, even though brief, might add up to some beginning steps toward improvement, and a degree of less aggressive behavior. It is interesting to see, with such a boy or girl, how he not only receives help from the calm and firm control of the cottage parent, but also, when group climate is good, from some of the individuals in the group who have been there for some time and have gone through a rugged period themselves. Such an older child (older in terms of length of stay or emotional development) may, during a temper outburst on the part of the younger one, or a barrage of strong language, make a comment such as, "Take it easy, kid," implying in his tone, "We understand how you feel, but it isn't necessary to carry on that way."

The too-quiet, withdrawn boy or girl may need help in being more self-assertive. This may be a discouraged boy, who perhaps is enuretic, not out-going, who feels inadequate at sports and activities at which other boys are able. It may be a sign of real progress when such a boy stands up and defends himself in a fight, or even becomes aggressive enough to haul off and hit another youngster (his own size or larger). It is important for a number of reasons that the cottage parent be informed of the child's life and experiences before coming into the group. In the area of discipline this will help the worker to avoid repeating a way of handling a child which may not have been the right way for him. The boy or girl may have a particularly sensitive area, which, when sparked off, causes an explosion. The cottage parent should know of these touchy spots beforehand so that previous mistakes will not be repeated. Children who come to institutions have often been punished by parents or others who had no real love for them. Such punishment, when vindictive, or isolated from any atmosphere of affection, raises in the child a deep sense of resentment, of unfairness, of wanting to strike back. The child who comes into the group may still be striking back at something which happened long before. He can accept punishment better from someone who means something to him, if it is fair, and when he receives, also, affection and acceptance from the person administering the punishment. Any disapproval should be disapproval of the act of the child and not of the child himself.

We must not forget the child who wishes to be punished and who provokes punishment in order to relieve his sense of guilt. He does this through aggressive, or as we sometimes say, acting out impulsive behavior (in contrast to the child who represses it). The guilt often stems from happenings previous to his coming to the institution, such as his feeling that he is somehow responsible for the separation and divorce of his parents, as well as from his inclination to think that he is "no good." He unconsciously seeks relief from this guilt by difficult behavior for which he will be punished. What he really needs is some casework or psychiatric help over a period of time so that some of the happenings of the past can be brought out and he can gain a degree of insight and understanding of what happened and why; that he is not responsible for his parents' behavior; that people do care about him. In other words, through individual help, some of these deep-seated feelings of guilt can be eased up and he does not have such an urge toward behavior for which he will be punished, which, in any case, gives him only temporary relief.

A housemother, in the course of a discussion on the subject of discipline, said, "Yes, but these children are different; they can't be handled as you would children in their own homes." Actually, the children are not different, but what has happened to them is different. The boy or girl in his own home has been taught, guided, and helped by his parents, step by step, year after year. The parents may have made mistakes—most parents do, somewhere along the line—but if their basic feeling of love for the child is right, then the mistakes will not affect the youngster too deeply. If the parents were too firm, or too lenient, at least they were on the whole consistent, and the child grew up in the same pattern. And then, too, and this is most important, he modeled after his parents, wanting to be like them. They set an example, and in this way established a standard of behavior for the child. All of this our child in the institutions has missed. Usually there was not a good, warm, secure parental image within the setting of a happy home, for the child to identify with. He may come into the group never having had an adult figure whom he admired and wanted to be like. Knowing of the many changes which children have usually experienced before coming to the institution, we can see that often there has been no consistency or continuity, no established sure way of living, The youngster has not had the opportunity to develop a sense of values, of right and wrong, of controlling impulsive behavior. The institution is charged with a grave responsibility and a real challenge as it tries to reeducate the child emotionally, and to give him adult figures with whom he will want to identify.

Hints and Suggestions

There can be no sure or pat answers about how to handle this or that problem. The following points are listed only as a place to start for further consideration and discussion. So much of the effectiveness of what is done depends on the climate of the group, the leadership, the former experiences and present progress of the child, and the philosophy and practices within a particular setting. Some of the points may suggest ways of helping to achieve a positive climate or a good spirit.

1. Do not allow children to destroy property, smash household or play equipment, or to physically hurt another child or adult. They need to know what the limits are, but should be allowed freedom and some choices within those limits. While outright destruction is controlled, we do have to accept the fact that there will be more replacement of windows, dishes, and repairs to bicycles, plumbing, etc., than in a family home.

2. Do allow for verbal expression, for example, for a child to be free to say he "does not like it here," or that he thinks a staff member is unfair or "mean." If he can get it out verbally and have a chance to talk it over, it saves a lot of resentment generally. If a child is bitter or sarcastic, do not retaliate with bitterness or sarcasm in manner or voice.

3. If a child is definitely testing you to see if you meant what you said, then stick to what you said.

4. Watch for behavior due to fatigue and make opportunities for the child who is difficult or irritable because he is tired to get some rest or to be alone for a while. With adolescent girls, watch for premenstrual tensions. A girl may be much more difficult at this time for physical reasons only, a condition for which medical help is now available.

5. Charts with stars, or elaborate systems of merits and demerits are really not good. It is not so easy to classify behavior; a child who is being very difficult may actually be making good personal progress. It is much better to depend on and use your relationship with the group rather than a chart or some artificial system. A new worker sometimes uses and needs a star chart as something to lean on until she gains strength and status on her job.

6. Recognize sheer animal spirits and physical exuberance, and allow for them. Give opportunities for bursts of activity, such as the time before the reading of a story and the actual going to bed.

7. Don't be "at" children too much for being dirty, biting fingernails, reading comics, chewing gum, or for lacking table manners. Overlook what you can, but when there is something serious, get to the bottom of it.

8. Do not, as a means of punishment, deprive the child of things he should be sure of and that we want him to feel he can count on, such as food and allowances.

9. You are trying to build up good work attitudes and habits. It is inconsistent, then, to assign extra work as punishment.

10. When you do punish a child, be sure that the punishment has some connection with the wrong-doing. If a child deliberately rides a bicycle into another child's, damaging both, it would be logical to deprive him of the use of the bicycle for a few days. The child who takes or destroys the toy of another member of the group may be asked to pay for it, or to replace it. If a boy or girl is overly noisy at the movies and has to be spoken to by the manager, then he stays home from the movies the next week. Dr. Morris Mayer advises that "two basic principles should be applied to all forms of punishment—it has to be logical and it has to be psychologically correct." *

11. The privilege of visiting at home for a week-end or Sunday should not be withheld as punishment. Whether or not a boy or girl visits his home is decided on a casework basis after careful study of the values of such a visit. This should be quite separate and apart from his good or poor behavior in the institution. Problems should be handled within their context and in the setting where they happened. The child's home situation is usually complicated in itself, and the child already confused by it. We should not compound confusion by making visits home dependent solely upon behavior within the institution.

12. Watch for those practices which may be a constant source of irritation, and see what adjustments can be made to change them, for example, youngsters being taken to school in a bus labeled with the name of the institution in large letters, or many groups of visitors being taken on tours through the buildings when the children are at home.

13. It's best not to compare one child unfavorably with another. The boy or girl may already have had a competitive relationship with a brother or sister, and to be matched up against the attainments of one of his peers and be found lacking will be of no help to him.

One could go on and add other do's and don'ts, and a staff of an agency should do just that. It is a good idea when mem-

* *A Guide for Child-care Workers* (New York, Child Welfare League of America, 1958).

bers of the institutional team put down in writing the principles and practices in which they have come to believe, ways
which they have tried and found to be effective and right for
the child rearing and treatment program within their particular
setting. Such a booklet of principles of "This is what we believe in" or "This is the guide for procedure for child care
staff in our institution" is extremely helpful to the new worker
who is not sure about what is expected of him or the children
in his group. It not only gives the new worker something to
go by, but it is also good for the worker who has been with the
agency for a longer period, to review from time to time.

The Use of Authority

The real authority should come from those who are the
closest to the children, the houseparents. The houseparent
makes the decisions and gives permissions for questions which
arise within the life of the group. This is all, of course, within
the framework of the overall program of the institution. As we
think of the cottage parent as the one in authority, it is well
when this person is strong in the eyes of the children, that he
can make sound decisions, grant permissions in the realm of
the daily life of the cottage.

Corporal punishment—spanking, slapping, hitting, forcing a
child to sit or stand alone in a corner for a long time—should
have no place in the modern child care agency. The adult who
is tempted to spank may do so to relieve his own feelings of
anger and exasperation, or after having been provoked by a
child. One child may provoke the houseparent to the point of
slapping or spanking in order to "get a rise" out of him, to get
attention, or to relieve his guilt when it is too overwhelming
to handle in any other way. Another child may have experi-

enced brutal beatings by parents who had no love for him and be terrified at the thought of the repetition of these experiences. English & Pearson * mention the three fears that children develop—fear of being deserted, of not being loved, and of being punished by physical mutilation. Most children coming into our institutions have already had the first two of these fears materialize and we can at least spare them the third. The houseparents in a large metropolitan area where children came from circumstances of extreme deprivation mentioned that new youngsters coming in usually quickly cleared with others in the group (not yet able to trust the new adults) as to "whether they hit you here." This fear of being struck evidenced itself as one of their uppermost anxieties as to what the new place would be like. Many houseparents do manage without ever using physical punishment. These are often the houseparents who are experienced, who have worked successfully with numbers of youngsters, and who have, through developing skill and understanding, handled many kinds of children and behavior very well. When children sense that such an experienced, capable adult also likes them very much and has a respect for their rights and for their dignity, their response is more likely to be a positive, nonprovocative one. And the adult is not so apt to feel that he needs to have the threat or actuality of physical punishment to fall back on.

The use of authority is good when its purpose is the best possible care, management, and direction of the children. If, on the other hand, authority is used by the worker to build up his own feeling of self-importance, or, as a child might say, "to throw his weight around," then the resentment of the group

* O. Spurgeon English and Gerald H. J. Pearson, *The Emotional Problems of Living* (New York, Norton, 1945).

is stirred up. Real authority comes when the members of the group have a sincere respect for the houseparent. This kind of authority does not come at once. It is acquired with successful experience, with time, and with knowledge. It often happens that the child gets a new idea of authority, or recasts his old conception of it. The authority which is fair and just, a part of a total climate where adults are making every effort to help youth toward growth and progress, is more acceptable and useable than authority combined with rejection or punishment and a general lack of affection. A boy or girl may welcome control or a good scolding which may be evidence to him that the adult really cares what he does or says, and wants to do something about it.

The staff member may, at times, feel caught between two different sets of values. On the one hand, a housemother will have certain personal standards. She likes a clean, nicely furnished house, good pictures, music, books, china, flowers. But she will have to live with rough language, derision, hostility, and boys and girls who have symptoms such as bed wetting, soiling, or unappetizing ways of eating. She will be called an Old Bag, Old Hag, Witch, or an Old Something Else. Cottage parents are sought who are warm, kindly people, who have a real affection for children, but at the same time they have to be able to let a lot of things run off like water off a duck's back. One housemother was called Old Hawk Eye, in quite a loving way. She usually could sense when something was brewing and even if one of her boys was not in sight but was up to something he should not be doing, she was somehow aware of it. Along with this awareness, she was a motherly person, liked by her boys. And when it came right down to it, they wanted her to be Old Hawk Eye, and to be able to control them, when necessary to be one jump ahead of them. The cottage parent needs to remind himself over and over that the bitter words, the angry accusations, the intense feelings, are not necessarily personal. The boy or girl *is* angry, about that there can be no doubt. But the source of his hostility may be in all of his past experiences. When these feelings come out they are directed toward the adult who is handy at the moment and that usually is the cottage parent.

The houseparent will always have some problems with individual children. Life will never be smooth and calm. Individuals have bad days, periods of dark moods, and spells of negative behavior. Monday, the day after parents have visited, or children have gone home for a day (or some have had no visitors or visits away), is usually a hard day. Conflicts over the home and parental situation are often stirred up again, and here it is important that the caseworker be available to the child to help him with what may have happened during the visit. There are days when the youngsters as a group do pretty well; other days when all are off-key. What is the balance to look for? Is it fair to say that the cottage parent should have more periods when the group response is positive, and the group is going along *with* the leader, than when they are negative? When the group is fighting the leader most of the time, there is something to worry about, and help should be sought from the administration and casework department to find out what is wrong and what can be done to make things better.

Problems in connection with difficult behavior loom larger and seem more overwhelming when the child care staff member feels stale on the job because he has been tied down to it too long without time off. The houseparent should not let the institution be his whole world. One needs opportunities to recover, to take in something new that is a complete change from child care, particularly the worker who has to give out so much. The cottage parent needs an interest outside of his work; to go to the movies, or a concert, to read, get out doors in the sun, go down town shopping, garden, or whatever his interests and inclinations may be. When rested and refreshed, to some degree at least, the problems and irritations may not seem as serious as they were after a long period on duty.

9. *Pets*

It was about ten o'clock in the evening when Claire, fourteen, literally barged into the office where the director sat alone doing some leftover paper work. On the desk in the "outgoing" mail basket a sleeping cat was curled up. Claire's group was late in getting settled that night, and the director had sensed the restlessness and irritability of the girls on the floor above, in the congregate building.

Claire's first words were, "You've got to let me go out for an hour and walk around and around some blocks, or I'll run away! I'm so sick and tired of this place, I can't stand it." The director knew well that Claire suffered keenly from the rejection of her mother, and that her feelings of guilt over the hostility which she felt toward her mother as the result were at times more than she could manage. One of her ways of meeting her problem was to run, and this impulse, set off tonight for some reason by a fight with another girl, was strongly on her now. She often walked and walked until she wore herself out, and one could see that at times she was so driven that she must get such relief. Tonight she also felt defiant, anticipating that an attempt might be made to keep her in. She was crying in an angry way, seeking air, movement, space, and relief from inner pressures.

The director said, "Before you go, just sit down here for a few moments, and tell me what happened upstairs." Claire sat reluctantly, poised for flight, on the very edge of her chair. She was offered Kleenex from the box on the desk. Somehow, this offer of a tissue to an adolescent girl often brought forth a flood of tears and nose blowing, together with harsh words— "this awful place—no one understands—we're so cooped up— I've *got* to get out!" The cat, her peace disturbed by Claire's raised voice and tension, got up, stretched, and looked at the girl, who reached out and took the animal into her lap. The director watched, hopefully. Fortunately the cat rearranged herself and settled heavily in Claire's lap. The girl stroked her and may have received a small degree of solace from the warm soft fur; the cat purred in response, with loud content. Claire talked of her immediate grievance but less defiantly, and gradually she calmed, but not completely, of course, because she never completely relaxed. But as long as the girl sat, well back in the chair now, and talked and sniffed, and was listened to by someone who gave full attention, and was almost held down by the sleeping heavy cat, each moment counted and perhaps she would not have to run after all. By eleven o'clock she was ready to go up to bed, and the director thought to herself, "It was the cat who did the trick."

Bill was a boy of twelve with a hard, tough exterior. His temper tantrums, rough language, and general what-do-I-care manner gave the impression of a boy who did not want and was not interested in receiving love. As he came home each day at lunch time, a certain little scene was often repeated. Sitting, usually in the same place, would be a small white and brown nondescript terrier known as Spot, who had real feeling of identification with his group. As Bill came along, obviously on the lookout for Spot, the dog ran to the boy, wagging not only his tail but his whole rear end, with the kind of a welcome only a dog can give. Bill knelt down, gathered Spot in his arms and there occurred a mutual exchange of love and devotion such as Bill would never in the world allow himself to show toward another being.

Pets can and do make such a positive and definite contribution to the life of a children's home that it sometimes almost seems as if they should be paid members of the treatment team because of all they add to the interest, life, warmth, and often humor of the group. Certainly the question of whether or not to have a pet, how many, and what kind of pets, should not be left to chance. This part of the program should be as carefully planned and worked out as some of the other aspects of treatment.

Many youngsters who come from crowded housing in big cities have never had the fun of living with a pet. We can give them this pleasurable new experience. One can think of many a natural family where the dog or cat has been, almost literally, one of the family, and as one of the family, beloved. In the same way, a pet may become an important member of the institutional living group. We are aware of those children who cannot love other children or adults, and who are afraid to allow themselves to show feelings of affection. Often they do allow themselves to love a pet, like Bill and his dog. Such a child may lavish the care on a pet that he himself would like to experience.

Pets—dogs in particular—actively *give* to children, of response, love, acceptance, even great devotion. A collie often feels responsible for protecting a group, or seeing that all members are present and accounted for. A pet can be of great help to the new child coming into the group. The boy or girl may turn to the animal, to stroke him, talk, and play with him, before he is able to make contact with or accept overtures of friendliness and welcome from the cottage parent or other children, or even before he interests himself in the available toys. Pets in evidence may be reassuring to the new child and his perhaps apprehensive parents.

A pet introduces humor, interest, and in some youngsters, feelings of protectiveness. A mother cat with kittens or a dog with puppies may evoke tenderness such as the child has not experienced before. For the child whose thoughts are mostly absorbed by his own anxieties, and who is concerned with himself almost completely, interest in a pet may take him out of himself to a degree and may help him to be concerned with another living creature.

It has sometimes been said that people who like children also have a special feeling for animals. Having a pet in a group does require that the group leader in charge must like animals, protect them from too much handling, and in the long run be responsible for their feeding and physical care as well as seeing that they have a chance to rest undisturbed. When a puppy or kitten is taken into a group there is the routine of house training and sometimes cleaning up, and the house-mother must be prepared to be responsible for this. Children take their cues from the group leader and will follow along with the example set by the adult who seriously concerns him-self with the well-being of the dog or cat. Children need to be taught how to care for an animal just as they are taught how to do other things.

However, there may be one or more individuals within a group with problems so severe that the group might not be ready for a pet unless it is a very large, strong, good-natured dog, able to look out for himself. It sometimes happens that the child who is filled with hostility may act out an uncontrollable hostile impulse toward a cat or bird or some other animal. It is important for the houseparent to understand the basis for such action, that the hostility which the child may be feeling toward someone in his past experience is being taken out on a defenseless animal. If the houseparent reacts with shock and is inclined to scold, shame, and punish the child, the youngster will feel guilty. This action on his part was, one might say, not done deliberately to hurt the animal, but stemmed from a much deeper impulse which the child was not able to control. Making him feel guilty is not going to help him.

What kinds of pets do we think of as making a real contribution to the life of a group? One finds more dogs than other animals, and the institution which has never before had pets and thinks of acquiring one often starts with a dog. This is sensible, for dogs like children, and many of them do very well in group living, particularly nonpedigreed dogs who are not high-strung, sensitive, or delicate. Short-haired terriers manage very well. A dog plays actively with children, often joins a play group and wants to take part. He goes along on picnics, attends parties, and may have his birthday or the day he arrived at the home recognized. It is a good idea to seek the advice of a veterinarian as to the type of dog, whether male or female, when looking for the first dog for a group or an institution.

It is easier for the dog or cat, and it is much more satisfactory for the children, when the pet belongs to a particular cottage group, rather than to the entire institution, or to a staff member personally. It is amazing to see how a pet will identify with a group. Even in the midst of a large and complicated cottage system, he knows very well where his home is

and who his children are. The children like this; there is so
much in their lives in the institution which they are required
to share with large numbers that there is much more satisfaction in the pet if he belongs exclusively to one particular group.
The housemother of the boys' group of which Bill and Spot
were members allowed this small dog to sleep on the boys' beds
at night, and the plan was that he rotated among members of
the group. He did not always wind up in the morning on the
same bed where he settled the night before, but this was accepted.

Cats are not really group animals by nature or by inclination. They do not like noise, confusion, milling around, great
activity, or change. A cat is not fond of relating to many personalities. However, some cats do manage to get along very
well under certain conditions. First of all, one cannot take a
sedate, middle-aged cat, one who has lived in a family home,
and suddenly thrust her into a group. Such a cat would be
terrified and frantic. Cats are at heart great individualists; they
get set in their ways and are much less adaptable than dogs.
It is best to introduce into the group a cat who was exposed
to children since she was a small kitten. Like children, the cat
who is most lovable and responsive is the one who has been
loved and cared for and who trusts adults. Pets dislike changes
in houseparents (particularly when a good houseparent leaves),
and they react negatively to such change just as children do.
They, too, need continuity and certainty in their lives.

There are animals who add interest and life but who are
not so much an active part of the group, or who are more
impersonal than cats and dogs. Canaries add a cheerful, colorful note. Budgie birds are very good; they like people. Rabbits
are appealing but cannot stand much handling and need care-

ful attention. Goldfish and turtles are popular, and children like to have them as their own personal possessions. When youngsters have sleeping rooms for one, two, three or four, this gives them the opportunity, which the smaller rooms afford, to have individual goldfish bowls, or a turtle in a pan. The mortality of goldfish is usually rather high, as they are greatly overfed, and children like feeding them more than they do changing the water. A housemother, describing Jimmie and his turtle, told of the bedtime hour when she always read a story or two to her boys' group after they were washed and in their pajamas. During the story period, Jimmie liked to take his turtle from its bowl, hold it in his hand or let it crawl up his arm or around on his pillow. He would be lost in reverie as he listened to the story and had a period of gentle play with his very own pet.

Other kinds of animals who appeal to children but whom adults are usually much less enthusiastic about are mice, hamsters, and snakes. A housemother of a small group of boys and girls around the age of six and seven told of her great wish and that of her group for a pet. But it was a rule of the Board under which she worked that there were to be no pets, an unreasonable rule to be sure, and one which the housemother hoped would soon be changed. On a visit to a day camp the children in this group managed to bring home a snake which they established in their doll house as its abode. It was a mild kind of a snake which submitted to being dressed up in a very small doll's bonnet from time to time.

Just as children ordinarily enjoy animals who are alive, so also do they like animal pictures as decorations for their rooms, dormitories, and along the hallways. Well-selected pictures of animals can do a good deal to promote an interest in, an acceptance toward, and a sympathy for animals. Boys usually like horses and smaller children respond to pictures of baby animals. There is a book called *Baby Animals* whose pictures might well be framed and used as decoration. Clare Newberry, who is famous for her studies of cats, kittens, and rabbits, has had published several portfolios of cat pictures, not expensive, and also suitable for framing.

10. Sex Attitudes and Education

Those phases of a child's life which have a direct or indirect bearing on the subject of sex, on boy-girl relationships, and on the role of the boy as a boy and the girl as a girl, are things which are at times a part of the youngster's thoughts and impulses, and over which he may have some real worries, questions, and concerns. Here the staff can be most helpful.

It is always well to know first what the boy or girl may have experienced previously that might indicate areas which require particularly sensitive help and special awareness on the part of the cottage parent. There are those youngsters who have seen and heard and lived with too much for their years and understanding. These are the children who come from physically crowded homes with too many members of a family squeezed into too few rooms. What the child has heard or seen may have raised unanswered questions and anxieties, or may even have been frightening. With others, such early experiences or observations may have been exciting or provocative. Some boys and girls have had parents who were unfaithful to one another. Such things become the basis for family quarrels, accusations, discussions by relatives, names called in anger, much of which the child may have observed and overheard with only a child's understanding of its meaning. Poor adult behavior often puts a stigma on the subject of sex, with the implication that the relationship between the sexes is something to be hidden, to be ashamed of, and which causes parents to fight, separate, and divorce.

If the child has been given no sex information by his parents (and often even when he has), he may have done some exploring or engaged in sex play in order to find out for himself. Perhaps rather than being helped, he was punished for this, or threats were made. With many families, the friendships of an adolescent girl with boys may cause the parents to be suspicious and to warn the girl continually that she "had better not get into trouble," thus putting the wrong light on her association with boys. Sometimes a mother who herself was pregnant before her marriage is unduly threatening toward her adolescent daughter. She may be projecting her feelings over her own experience and guilt on to her daughter. One often finds in placement, too, the girl who has had little parental love, and who has always felt unwanted. In her need for affection she may turn to boys at an earlier age, or more aggressively, than the average girl. She permits sex play or extreme "necking" which bring her attention and make her popular with a certain type of boy, giving her, from boys, the acceptance she has not received from adults. Because of their earlier experiences, boys and girls who come into the institution may have built up more negative than positive information as well as a confused emotional response to the subject of sex.

It is of the utmost importance, therefore, that the staff not repeat any attitudes of suspicion or condemnation, nor give the idea that curiosity, sex play, or masturbation are to be hushed, hidden, repressed, and warned against. With an honest, open, direct, and straightforward attitude that the facts of life are something which the child learns about just as he learns about other subjects, the houseparent can give the youngster a good deal of reassurance and often relief. The child often may need re-education rather than new knowledge, to be freed first of the troublesome attitudes which he may have absorbed, the incorrect information he has picked up and the anxiety feelings which have developed as a result, before he is ready to understand and accept on a new and fresh basis.

Some of the specific questions which are important for the houseparent to consider pertain: 1) to the information which children seek and are interested in at different ages, who should give this, and when; 2) to how to deal, or not to deal, with sex play and masturbation, and 3) to the positive approach toward boy-girl relationships.

What Do They Want to Know?

Growing boys and girls need, and usually seek, knowledge in these areas: anatomical differences between boys and girls; curiosity about the appearance and functions of the sexual organs, as well as the whole body; relations between the sexes; how babies are conceived and born; all of the changes and surge of feelings which arise in adolescence; the preparation of girls for menstruation; and finally, both boys and girls sometimes need reassurance about their own development, particularly when they feel they are not as physically mature as they should be. It is usually the younger children who want to know about babies and being born. As they grow toward adolescence, they seek information such as found in *The Facts of Love and Life for Teen-Agers.** But we must always keep in mind that the boy or girl coming into the group at adolescence may have missed the earlier "being born" information, and may want to go back and learn more about that too. Often adolescents who

* By Evelyn Millie Duval (New York, Popular Library, 1957).

sometimes have a know-it-all attitude, and who like to give the impression that they are more experienced than they actually are, are really quite naive about physiology and bodily functions. And it should not only be the accurate information and correct vocabulary that they receive, but hopefully, a matter-of-fact and shockproof attitude on the part of the staff member as well. Even though a boy or girl may know something about any of the areas mentioned above, it is well for him to be told about it again by the houseparent or caseworker. In some cases he would like to hear your version in order to test the validity of what he has previously heard, or he may want to see how knowledgeable you are, how you handle this. If he asks the same question a second or third time, remember that perhaps the first time he did not take it in. Maybe he had a longer, more involved explanation than he asked for, or a blocking due to previous experiences or attitudes may have stood in the way of his really listening, understanding, or remembering. No matter what his motive for seeking further information, or for asking again what we think he already knows, the houseparent has an opportunity to let the young child or the adolescent know that he can be easily approached for discussion on this subject. The interest of the housemother is reassuring to a girl as the housemother helps her prepare for menstruation, not only in the practical aspects of getting the necessary belt, pads, etc., in readiness for her well beforehand, but also in talking with her about any questions she may have. Again, the girl may need an adult interpretation or explanation of this function, which she may not have had beforehand.

BOOKS AND PAMPHLETS. There is a good selection of books and pamphlets available, dealing with children's questions and the information they often seek at different ages. These books are directly helpful to the houseparent who reads them and is familiar with their contents. They explain things in a language which a boy or girl can understand, and the adult reader can learn much from the approach of these authors who have made a thorough study of the content material as well as the best way of presenting it to a boy or girl of today. The child who may not be able to read may want to look at the pictures and have the contents read or explained to him. And then, of course, there is the child who wants to read the book himself, but who would like to discuss it later, or who may have additional questions.

A child care staff member needs to have certain basic working equipment, and books of various kinds are a part of this. It is a good plan to have, in the room or apartment of the cottage parent, the books for youth on sex education that are best suited to the age of his particular group. In addition to this literature, there will be other reference books which the cottage parent and group use together, for example, those on craft activities, a dictionary, and others, so that the subject of sex is not set apart as something special but that the written material dealing with it is a part of any of those reference books which the child and worker share.

Story books which youngsters read for pleasure should be in the living room or elsewhere, where they are available to all in the cottage or dormitory at all times. Special reference books, such as those just mentioned, might be kept in the cottage parents' own rooms, but be given out freely on request, or the suggestion made that the boy or girl might like to look them over to know they are there in case he later wants to use them. This arrangement makes it possible for the adult to be aware of the interest in these books on the part of the individuals within the group. When they are on the bookshelf of the cottage parent, this suggests that their use will involve the child-houseparent relationship, since the worker will be drawn in, to a more or less degree, as the books are used by the child. It also says to the child, "These books are here for you when you want to use them; these are good books, and this is an acceptable subject that we expect you will be interested in."

An agency might feel that one set of books or pamphlets on the subject of sex education might serve the needs of all of the groups, to be kept perhaps in a central library and drawn out as needed. But this kind of use does present limitations. There are psychological moments which are then lost, that is, the times when a child comes with his questions, or asks for an explanation. The right moment is then. If the cottage parent has to wait until the next day and go to the central library, he may find that the particular book he is seeking is not in, and in the subsequent wait for it, the appropriate time slips by. And it will be found, too, that in institutions having groups of even eight to ten children, there will be enough use made of a collection of four or five books and pamphlets to justify a set for each group. It will be possible, also, to select different reading material for various departments with particular age groups in mind. When these books are close enough to the child's daily life to be within sight, this invites their use when the impulse is upon the child to seek out something he wants to know.

SEX EDUCATION INDIVIDUALLY AND IN GROUPS. There are times when a child wants a private conversation and can best be helped individually, and other times when the group can be used effectively for discussion. When the children have had varying experiences, different backgrounds, scattered and sometimes even distorted information, and represent a wide age span, it may be difficult to gear a group discussion to the needs of all members. When sex information is "given out" in a sort of teacher-student relationship in a group session, or to several groups together, there may be the inclination to think that now the subject of sex has been dealt with once and for all and "we have had our lessons on sex education." But it doesn't work that way. New children are constantly coming into the groups. And the youngster does not learn about sex all in one session but rather, a bit at a time, as much as he wants at the moment and is ready for. As teaching, it should not be imposed on those members of the group who may just then not have any special interest. It is not a sporadic but rather an on-going part of the program.

On the other hand, there are some children who would not feel free to ask questions or to seek explanation on their own initiative because of early experiences or observations which may have caused them to feel that the subject was an unacceptable one. In a group where the climate is good and discussion free, the fearful individual may be more comfortable when lost in the group, so to speak. In this connection, a housemother told this story. Her girls, ten of them, were in bed, relaxed and rather mellow after she had read them a story. The dormitory was dark except for one light at the table where the housemother sat. She continued to sit there, and there was some chatting among the girls and housemother of this and that. Then, from a far corner, Inez, aged around twelve or thirteen, asked, "Mrs. Hoffman, is it true when a baby is born that the mother spits it out? My mother keeps telling me that." Mrs. Hoffman knew that Inez was old enough and sophisticated enough to know how babies are born, and she did not know the reason why Inez asked this question at this point in all seriousness. However, she gave a direct and informative answer. Further questions and comments came out, and Anna-Marie, on her bed, covered her head with a pillow. Anna-Marie had recently come from a European country as a refugee, and this kind of discussion was new to her and made her uncomfortable. But the housemother noticed that while the pillow covered the girl's face, Anna-Marie had not pulled it over her ears, and was listening intently to everything said. Sometimes a group discussion springs up quite spontaneously and unplanned in this way. There it is, and the houseparent handles it.

WHO OF THE STAFF SHOULD ANSWER QUESTIONS? The child may bring his questions, or something which is bothering him, either to the cottage parent or to the caseworker, or, if he is receiving psychiatric treatment, to the psychiatrist. A housemother of a group of adolescent boys may not feel as capable of discussing this subject as a male caseworker, group worker, or some other male member of the staff with whom a boy might feel he could be more direct. In the youngster's periods with the caseworker, there may be natural opportunities to help a boy or girl in relation to his past or present experiences, and again, the area of sex is related to his total situation. It may be tied up with some of the conflicts with which the worker is trying to help him, and not necessarily set apart as an isolated subject. The cottage parent may, in his observations of the child in the group, become aware of something which is bothering him. These observations are then shared with the caseworker who has opportunities in the periods spent with the child to go into things more thoroughly. The case of Joan illustrates this.

Joan joined a group of ten girls when she was eleven, following her father's desertion and her parents' divorce. Her mother, who was to be financially and otherwise responsible for the girl, returned to work. She was conscientious about paying for the board, kept her daughter well clothed and often had Joan to spend Sundays and some week-ends with her in her small apartment. When Joan was fourteen, her mother planned to remarry and take the girl home. The prospective step-father was fond of Joan, and the couple often devoted their Sunday afternoons to some activity which she liked. Sometimes the three were together in the mother's apartment.

Joan, however resisted the idea of returning home and seemed to have no pleasurable anticipation of the move. The reasons for her lack of enthusiasm puzzled both her mother and the caseworker to whom Joan was unable to tell what was bothering her. Then one evening Joan, with some other members of her group, was watching a play on television. During an ardent love scene, she rose in anger and shouted, "I *hate* that love making, and all that kissing!" With this, she dashed to her room in angry tears to escape the play and the television. The housemother wisely did nothing about the outburst at that moment other than to accept Joan's statement as one of the critical comments the girls often made about various plays and programs. But the housemother did tell the caseworker of the incident and this gave the latter a clue as to Joan's resistance to returning home.

In one of her subsequent interviews with the girl, the caseworker helped Joan to tell of her feelings of embarrassment and hesitancy in living with the newly married couple as closely as would be necessary in her mother's apartment where they would be for several months until a larger place was available. Because of the mother's own understanding and general helpfulness, the caseworker was able to discuss with her this phase of the girl's return, and as a result, Joan stayed on in the cottage group for several more months until the family could move into a larger apartment. This additional time allowed, also, for Joan to spend some Sundays at home, and thus more gradually to become prepared for her introduction to the new living arrangement.

Whether it is the staff member who talks with a child individually, or the one who leads a group discussion, this can be accomplished more effectively by the worker who has a good and well-established (over some period of time) relationship with the child or with the group. The boy or girl finds it easier to talk with the person whom he likes and in whom he has confidence. He must feel sure that he will not be criticized and that the adult will not be shocked by what he tells or what he asks, also, that he will not be put off with, "We'll talk about that another time."

Some youngsters come to the cottage parent for general information and to the caseworker for more specific help in relation to themselves, their family situation, or their own actual experiences. There is little danger that too many people on the staff will become involved; in fact, the opposite is more often true, that this area of the child's education is not handled at all, or only superficially. One still finds too often the situation where everyone is waiting for another person on the staff to take care of this part of the job.

Masturbation, Exploration and Sex Play

One of the most frequent questions raised by houseparents concerns masturbation, which is in evidence more or less in most groups. Masturbation is something which almost every normal child goes through and then grows past. The boy or girl who has been deprived of love and personal attention and affection may masturbate excessively, turning to himself for comfort and pleasurable feeling. Dr. Irene Josselyn puts it this way: "One child may utilize masturbation as another might utilize thumb sucking, as a way of creating pleasant internal feelings when the external world is too lonesome or too ungratifying." *

The boy or girl who masturbates a good deal may have severe feelings of guilt about it, or fear self-injury of some sort. A housefather told of an incident when he found some of the boys in his group masturbating. As he spoke with the boys, telling them he knew they had been masturbating, he said, "I wonder if you have some questions about this you would like to ask. If you do, let's talk about it." He reported an immediate response from the boys with specific questions: "Will it hurt me? Will I lose my brains? Will I be able to get married? Does your stomach run all out? Will I run dry?" The housefather thought the main theme had been about the feelings of loss. He answered the boys in terms of masturbation being an activity which most boys did at some time or other, some more than others, and also that one who did not know enough about it could get ideas that were not true. In answer to their specific fears, the housefather told what the liquid was, of which only a few drops came out, its purpose, and how it was replenished by nature.

Two boys from another institution were picked up by two policemen in a public park at dusk, engaged in mutual masturbation. The police brought them home to their cottage and asked to speak to whoever was in authority. The male case-

* *The Happy Child* (New York, Random House, 1955).

worker who had been working with both boys happened to be around, and the housemother called him over. One of the policemen had threatened to take the boys to court, called them perverts, and said that the law takes care of such boys. The second officer commented that he did not think it was anything to make such a fuss about, that he knew it was not abnormal, but that the boys needed some help from the caseworker. The worker did talk with the boys together and individually at the time and in subsequent periods with them. The housemother made no particular comment to the boys on their return, leaving the specific handling of the situation to the caseworker.

One of the boys, aged thirteen, was troubled by the fact that he was rather obese; he was worried about his "baby fat," his bed wetting, occasional thumb sucking, his small penis, and the fact that he was not accepted by the other boys. All together, this boy was seriously concerned that there was something wrong with him, and needed a good deal of reassurance. The caseworker not only saw him once a week during their regular appointments, but also showed a friendly interest in him in their casual meetings on the campus. Among other things, he talked with him about the difference in the rate of development of different boys, and that size actually had little to do with being adequate as a masculine person. With time, this boy made good progress, and came closer to seeing himself as one who could, and did, take more active part in sports. The other boys gradually lost interest in him as a boy they could tease and bait. While he did continue to wet his bed all during his stay in the group, until the age of fifteen, this had almost completely disappeared at twenty. He kept in touch with his housemother after he left the institution, and she was pleased at his satisfactory adjustment. After graduating from high school, he got a good job as a radio and TV repair worker, at which he did very well. He acquired a car, grew tall, and lost the excess weight and earlier soft appearance.

This case points up, too, the danger of putting a strong label on a boy or girl, as the one policeman did with this boy, because of one incident. This is sometimes done to the child who steals, too, or the one referred to as a "bedwetter," and it is something to be avoided. The way in which one specific incident, as the one in which the two boys were involved, is handled may well affect a child's entire future.

In the past there used to be a disproportionate amount of concern over, and wary watching for, possible sex play, together with undue alarm when anything of this nature was observed. This fearfulness was reflected in the widespread practice of planning sleeping rooms for three children rather than two, the thought behind this being that if two children engaged in sex play, the third would bring word of it to a staff member. The tendency toward sleeping rooms for three was so strong that the limitations of this arrangement in other respects were overlooked.

Nowadays there is a more general understanding and acceptance of the fact that a certain amount of curiosity, sex play, and masturbation is usual, and that it is nothing to moralize over, or cause to remove a child from the institution. Group life has a definite advantage over some other situations where the child is alone much of the time. In the groups, so much of interest and stimulation can be offered along the lines of play activities and equipment that the child can find enough satisfactions in the life around him to keep him busy and interested. The fact that he can be given a good deal of personal attention from a number of adults goes hand-in-hand with the activities provided. Boys and girls actively swimming and playing in a pool together on a summer afternoon, screaming and splashing, will not necessarily be thinking of sex play; nor will a group of boys on the baseball field, with a leader they look up to.

And here again, the size of the group is important and plays a distinct role as it does in so many other aspects of care. A child care staff member with a small group, and with the time, patience, and energy (*because* the group is small) can make bedtime a satisfactory period by giving each child personal attention, can provide a story or other interesting bedtime activities, and not send the group off to bed too early or too abruptly—thus helping the child to settle down and go to sleep. In contrast, when there is a large group and more regimentation is necessary, when the group is sent off to bed too much on its own and too perfunctorily, one might find a greater amount of masturbation, the lonesome, wide-awake child turning to comfort himself because his way of life as arranged and managed for him is too impersonal and does not satisfy and support him.

Boy-Girl Relationships

THE COEDUCATIONAL INSTITUTION. The agency which provides care for both boys and girls in the same setting has a real opportunity in the area of boy-girl relationships. When an institution offers care only for girls or for boys, the members of the opposite sex may assume a glamor and desirability out of all proportion to reality, the objects of much fantasy and wishful thinking. When boys and girls live on the same campus with many opportunities for companionship and joint activities, they are more matter-of-fact and down-to-earth about each other. There are many occasions to select and make friends. In one way or another—going to school, playing on the same grounds, sometimes sharing the same dining room, being together at picnics and parties, going to the movies, meeting again and again on the campus, in blue jeans or dressed in their best—boys and girls have contacts under various circumstances, casually or as companions, friends and playmates. A youngster may feel a kind of a bond with his peers in the institution because of the mutual experience of living together in a specialized kind of residence for youth, different from that which he has with others in the community public school. Often the social occasions offered in institutions, and the opportunities for many contacts with members of the opposite sex, both staff and children, gives a boy or girl confidence with others of his age in the community.

However, one of the distinct advantages of the cottage system is that boys and girls, particularly of preadolescent and adolescent age, can be housed in separate units. Living in dormitories in the same congregate building increases the need for supervision, and has proved too provocative in some cases, leading to incidents of sex relations between adolescent boys and girls housed under one roof.

We have mentioned the feeling of self-depreciation and lack of self-worth which bothers many boys and girls in institutions. They are nagged persistently by the thought that because of what has happened to them and their families, they are not as good as youngsters who live in a more settled way in intact homes. Their sensitivity affects their natural inclinations to seek out, for friendships, members of their own as well as the opposite sex. A boy living in an institution and going to a community school may think he is not good enough for a girl in one of his classes, whom he likes. Or, he may think that if he makes overtures of friendship toward her, he will be rebuffed, and he is not willing to take a chance that this may happen. The setting in which he is living is making an attempt, through activities, staff attitudes, and in all phases of its philosophy and program, to give him a feeling of self-worth, that he is good and well thought of. In such an atmosphere he feels safe in his casual and social contacts with the girls in other groups, to test out his own feelings for them, and of them toward him, and this gives him some self-assurance. If several girls in the institution find him attractive and indicate that they would like a closer friendship with him, this gives him more self-confidence and courage in relation to the girl at school on whom *he* has his eye.

There is often substantial worry that if the institution allows a good deal of freedom in outside contacts, the adolescent girl may become pregnant. This may cause the staff to be overly rigid in denying dating privileges, or other community activities, such as part-time work opportunities. The fear that something may happen to a girl is tied up with the staff's feeling that they will then have failed with her, and also that this is a reflection on the reputation and standing of the agency. It is true that an adolescent girl who has great need for affection in her life generally, or perhaps for other reasons, may be too aggressive with boys, provocative, and quite willing to "go all the way." Sometimes those who take care of boys feel that the adolescent girl leads a boy on too fast, that the girls are more knowing than are boys of their same age, and that it is the girls who are in the main responsible for situations which lead to difficulty. While it is hoped that an institution can give an adolescent girl enough help so that she will eventually and in good time make a happy and stable marriage, we must remember that unmarried motherhood is more usual with girls who have not had secure homes and where there have been psychological difficulties between the parents, and the parents and the girl. When a girl becomes promiscuous, this is not an indication, as is often erroneously said, that she is "boy crazy" or "over-sexed." The problem goes much deeper than that.

It is better to allow the girls in the average institution to date, to attend planned and supervised boy-girl parties within the agency, and to be helped by the housemother as they make mistakes in makeup, dress, conduct, and in coming home on time. This is how they learn. The girl who has been too closely held in may, when she finally leaves the institution, seek too intensively for all that she feels she has missed. Often, within a group, girls are critical of one another's actions in a constructive way. The group may point out to one of its members that she was loud, or acting silly, or something of the sort, which she will usually take in much better spirit than if the criticism came from an adult.

One of the most usual complaints heard when girls date "outside" boys is in regard to the difficulty of getting them to come home at the hours decided upon. Even though the girl and her date may have agreed with the houseparent that she be back by 11 or 12, and *no later*, the girl may be urged by the group she is with to stay out just a little longer, and she may appear, with convincing excuses, at 11:30 or 12:15. Here it is quite logical for the housemother to deny her a dating privilege for the next night when she would normally have been allowed to go out. (This point is discussed in the chapter on discipline.) The housemother who cooperates with the girls and works carefully with them on their dating privileges, who waits up fully dressed and on the job until all have returned, should be firm and consistent on checking-in time. There will always be some who will test out the rule but they can accept it, and can accept being kept in for an evening if they break the rule, if other aspects of the dating are reasonable. Although the girls may complain at the time that the staff member is unfair, they do, in the long run, want to have certain limits adhered to.

Girls who live in a coeducational setting often prefer, as more attractive to those on the campus, boys who live on the outside. They usually like boys, too, who are older than they are, and sometimes consider the boys of their own age living in other cottages as quite young and unsophisticated. Boys who date girls from the community are able to leave the institution behind them for a few hours. Teen-age girls, on the other hand, may go through adolescent agonies in the process of dating boys from the outside. In their natural tendency to exaggerate many of their emotions, they suffer, wondering what this boy will think of them for living in a children's Home. How will the cottage parent receive him when he comes to call for her? (Even good, thoughtful, natural parents of a girl in her own home find they can never achieve the exacting requirements set by their daughter at a time like this; she may be mortified by them, no matter how hard they try.) And the teen-age girl living in a group has not just one small brother or sister to worry about, but what may seem to her like hundreds of curious and giggling little girls surrounding her.

When the cottage mother, sensitive to the great importance this occasion has for a girl, greets the boy friend graciously, and has cleared the scene of other youngsters, it can be made into a positive experience which will be of great help to a girl. The attitude of the cottage parent which implies, "We think well of this girl," is carried over to the boy and his responsibility. A girl's own sense of self-esteem can be observed in her choice of boys as friends. As she is helped to gain a deeper sense of self-worth, she grows to feel that she is good enough for a boy of good standards, and that she can be selective, and that she can wait.

Institutions are trying in many different ways to make it possible for the adolescent boys and girls in their care to have opportunities for good friendships. For example, Mr. and Mrs. M., social workers by profession, were responsible for a residence for twenty-five adolescent girls who attended seventh and eighth grade and high school. Many of the girls had been in placement most of their growing-up years, and they presented the whole range of difficulties which one might find with such a group. However, they were able to attend community schools, with many contacts and conferences on the part of the agency caseworker and the schools. The girls were allowed to have dates within reason, depending on the history and adjustment as well as the length of stay of the individual, and other factors which needed to be taken into consideration.

The director, Mr. M., told of his plan for Sunday afternoons. Although he had a family of his own, Mr. M. devoted each Sunday afternoon to the group, most of whom had no Sunday visitors, and only a few of whom went home to visit. Sunday was the day when the girls could invite boys to the Home for the afternoon and early evening. Although this was a Home located in the city, there was a good-sized back yard with a fireplace and some lawn games. One of the things eagerly awaited was an early supper of hamburgers and sausages, to which the boys were invited, and which the boys and girls prepared together. The fact that these boys from the community were regularly on the grounds in this way gave the director a chance to know them, and to know them in relation to the girls whom they were dating. It also showed the boys that the director was interested in, and concerned with, the girls as well as being protective of them. It did something for the girls to know that their boy friends actually enjoyed these Sunday afternoons on the grounds, or in cold weather, in the living room or recreation room. Helpful, of course, was Mr. M.'s ability to get along with the boys, to make them feel comfortable, and to set a good example for them by his conduct and manner.

FOR THE HOUSEPARENT'S BOOKSHELF

Duvall, Dr. Evelyn Millis. *Facts of Love and Life for Teen-Agers.* New York, Popular Library, 1957. 35¢

Levine, Dr. Milton and Jean Seligman. *A Baby Is Born.* New York, Simon and Schuster, 1949.

——. *The Wonder of Life.* New York, Simon and Schuster, 1952. *What to Tell Your Children About Sex.* New York, Child Study Association of America, 132 East 74th Street, New York 21. 35¢

11. Religion

One of the strongest heritages transmitted from parents to child, from generation to generation within a family, is that of belonging to a certain faith, being members of a church, and observing together the teachings of their religion. Many children who grow up in their own homes experience, as they follow the religious practice of their parents, grandparents, and greatgrandparents, an additional sense of belonging and of continuity, as members of a church which is a vital force in any community. The spiritual life of the child is closely tied up with his relationships with his parents and other relatives. He begins early to imitate, to absorb, and then to practice the spirit and ways of religious observances in his family and in his church. In the case of a family which has lived for a long time in one community, it may happen that the same priest, rabbi, or minister who baptized the child, will also officiate at his confirmation, first communion, or other rites, and later, at his marriage and the baptism of his children. Even when there are changes in the religious leader, these observances take place within the same church to which the family belongs.

The boys and girls who are in the care of child placement agencies have missed this continuity. The on-going course of their lives—family life, school, Sunday School, or church—has been interrupted by shattering experiences, with broken relationships all along the way, together with moves from one community or neighborhood to another. The institution has the opportunity with some children, to introduce them to religious observances, and with others, to help them pick up and renew services in familiar religious surroundings. They may be helped to gain a little of the feeling that while other things change, their church does remain constant. These youngsters need something to believe in, to build up faith in, again, to hang on to. With many, their first introduction to the saying of grace before meals, the bedtime prayer, attending Sunday School, singing in the choir, or becoming a member of a young people's church group, may come in the new setting.

Churches of all denominations, feeling a real sense of responsibility for children separated from their families, have, throughout the years, established many of the agencies providing foster homes and institutional care, in an earnest effort to provide for those of their faith. Agencies which receive children of various faiths are conscientious about bringing the religious leaders of all denominations to the children, or making use of community facilities. Each faith has its own beliefs and goals for the children and staff, as well as its convictions about what should be expected and taught and the procedure of the teaching. Whatever the form or practice of this religious belief, the climate of the institution and the spirit of the staff, the degree of staff understanding and devotion to children, is of the utmost importance. Good climate and staff spirit do much to nourish the practices and observances of the agency, no matter what its affiliation. We will consider, in this chapter, religious practices from the standpoint of the houseparent and what he or she does to help the child within the framework of the agency.

There is a good opportunity within any group to bring meaning to some of the spiritual aspects as they are integrated into daily life and the general program. One such observance, usually found in all institutions, is the saying of grace before meals. As one rather typical group, made up of highly geared, outgoing, often noisy and occasionally obstreperous children, was observed, it did manage to become quiet for a moment or two before each meal. When the dining room bustle had hushed, the children said together one short simple grace or another, such as, "For food and friends and Father's love, we thank thee." The newly admitted boy or girl first watched and listened and then took part. The youngsters in the dining room might not seem impressed with, or in awe of, any member of the staff or any other part of the program or practice, but this brief moment when everyone, for once, was quiet, always carried an overtone of dignity and a small element of reverence, which lifted the group out of its noisy everyday life. It was good, during the day, to have the repetition of these three moments. The children might, at one time or another, complain about or resist any other part of the routine; about grace before meals there was never a complaint. Naturally some, during the short prayer, might be eyeing with pure physical anticipation, the mashed potatoes and gravy, or a roving eye might be checking to see what the dessert would be, or perhaps the small grace was said mechanically part of the time, but still it became part of a way of life, perhaps not known to the child before.

Going to Sunday School is something that most youngsters do. And because children living in institutions like to do what other children are doing, they too need and often welcome a chance to attend Sunday School. Like going to regular school, to camp, belonging to the Scouts or another community group, there is a reassuring normalcy about going to Sunday School. It also contributes another accent to the week.

In institutions caring for disturbed or delinquent boys and girls, some may not be able to attend community churches or Sunday Schools. As many Sunday School teachers are untrained volunteers, they may not understand or be able to manage children presenting special difficulties. In such cases, as well as others where a youngster cannot fit in comfortably or be completely welcome in a general Sunday School, a plan for having such services within the institution might be better, just as an inside school arrangement often needs to be made.

In any phase of child care, we cannot expect that all of the children will be able to fit into the same pattern or program. Spiritual help also needs to be considered on an individual basis, and must proceed at the pace of the individual. Services and lessons should not be too long. When periods of devotional services are too drawn out, children reach a point where they take nothing in. And we remember here again, that the attention span of children in placement is often even shorter than that of the average child. They are inclined to be more than normally restless and impatient, and until their general adjustment has improved, they are not able to stick to many things—play, school, or religious observances, for more than short periods of time.

After attending Sunday School, some boys and girls go on to their first communion, or confirmation. Just as graduation from grade or high school marks the achievement of a certain goal, so this special religious step represents growth in the direction of choice and belief in church affiliation. For the adolescent, the church offers, too, youth groups, choir, and other activities which give him opportunities to become acquainted with and share in activities with other young people in the community.

As with so many of the things we keep in mind when we consider all of the needs of the child first admitted to care, we remember, with religious practice, also to proceed slowly. For the child who has had little or no introduction to religious observances of any kind, the houseparent must not expect too much of him too quickly. The child must not be overwhelmed or forced. Spiritual feeling, understanding, and belief cannot flourish on a hard and fast insistence on ritual or chapel and church attendance alone.

Some will say that just as a pattern is set within an institution whereby a child is expected to nourish his body with food and his mind with education, so should a pattern of daily religious observance of some kind lead him to spiritual nourishment and education. One institution director said that a child is not to be forced to take part in daily chapel exercises, but rather that these exercises are integrated into the pattern of living so that the children just take it for granted. Whether it is such a taken-for-granted regular practice which is part of a way of life, or even the more casual practice of another institution, it flourishes better when the total climate is good. Monsignor Joseph Springob, of Milwaukee, says, in this connection: "The means which the institution can use most effectively for the religious growth of the child seems to me to be its climate. This climate is as unobstrusive and as beneficial to the religious growth of the child as it is to the child's mental health. Most important is an attitude of love on the part of the adults. Such love is composed of many parts: warmth, genuine concern for children, mercifulness, forgiveness, fairness, honesty—honesty in the sense of being and acting what one claims to be. Unfortunately many do not love other human beings to the degree and in the manner that their professed love of God requires."

As we consider a little further the thought that it is better to take it slowly, and to have the youngster build up faith and belief gradually, when he is ready for it, the case of Ruth offers a good example. Ruth, who had no parental ties, was in a nondenominational children's home as a small child and again in her high-school years, with an interval of care in a relative's home between. As a little girl Ruth went regularly to Sunday School and liked it. However, in her teens, she had no interest in church activities, and although she was encouraged to attend, this was not insisted upon. After graduating from high school and working for a time, she made a happy marriage, in which she found not only a good husband, but a mother as well, in her husband's mother. When she was twenty-five, she discussed her present happiness, her three children, her husband's interest in them, their love of one another, and their family life. In addition, she had joined the church of her husband's family's faith: both happened to be Protestant. This, she said, had given her, more than ever, a feeling of belonging, of being members of their church and community.

The timing of Ruth's interest in a church connection suggests the possibility that some of the spiritual practices to which the children are exposed and in which they take part may not seem to mean too much to them at the time, but it is something which may have begun to lay a foundation for a later time and interest. Ruth's housemother did not insist on regular church attendance during the girl's high-school years, when she was upset over a good many things. Now later, religion was something which she herself sought out because she wished to do so, and it had great meaning and significance to her as a part of her good family life, happier adjustment, and growing maturity. In other words, the institution sows some seeds of spiritual thoughts, beliefs, knowledge, and practice, but must recognize that at first they may not seem to take root because the soil in which they were planted was not able to nourish them, and that they may not grow until many years later when conditions are right for their growth.

The houseparent can give meaning to many of the spiritual aspects of living, as he helps the child to weave these into the things he does and sees every day. There are a number of ways this can be done. The housemother who reads or tells stories to her group may include a Bible story from time to time. Mentioned later, in connection with Christmas, are the possibilities inherent in planning and acting out the Christmas story. Christmas hymns and carols as they are learned, and sung, or heard on records are another way of emphasizing the real spirit of Christmas. Most boys or girls will like to see a baby baptized, or a wedding, either in a church or at home. So often children have heard of, or experienced within their own relationship, the hasty justice-of-the-peace marriage, and to observe a wedding service in a church will give a different picture and create a new impression. This experience has added meaning when the child is acquainted with the participants in the wedding or baptismal ceremony.

A growing knowledge and appreciation of God can be built up too, through a simple introduction to astronomy and a general appreciation of nature and outdoor things. In the rush and accelerated tempo of the atomic age, there has been all too little time, interest, and leadership to help children to observe, to know, and to appreciate the details, the purpose and plan of the wonders and beauties of nature. These things have great spiritual meaning also.

There can be dangers as well as positive values in the religious practices of an institution. Because of the feelings of guilt which many children in placement are already troubled with, we must be careful that the approach of the religious part of the child's life does not carry strong concepts of punishment. Confused ideas of sin, and what being sinful means, only add to the anxiety and discomfort of the child. Reverend Arnold Purdie, in his chapter, "Religion in Institution Living" carries this thought a little further when he says: "The presentation of a stern vindictive and punishing God demands the repression of human urges and desires and may result in the development of guilt and anxiety. The picture of an avenging God may cause serious disturbance in a child who is trying to learn to handle such impulses as hostility toward his parents, or strong sexual desires." *

An authority in still another faith makes an additional important point as to the setting in which the child best experiences faith. Reverend Benjamin Gjenvick, Director of the Lutheran Welfare Society of Wisconsin, says: "Religion can easily be reduced to irrelevent sentimentality. There is little point in telling a child who feels worthless, who has not known love, that God loves him. This is to mock the child and to mock God. The child requires first a demonstration of what God's love is like when it comes through a person. Once he has an experience of another person's closeness, the care and

* *Creative Group Living in a Children's Institution* (New York, Association Press, 1951).

concern of God for him may begin to be more than hollow words. The word about God must be wrapped in human deeds of care, concern, understanding, discipline and love. Faith and friendship with God may grow as faith and friendship with other people become possible for a child."

Damage also results when the religious counselor offers advice without having sufficient knowledge of the child's history or capacities, or when he gives guidance at variance with the treatment goals of the institution. The caseworker, as far as confidentiality permits, might well discuss a child's reactions, needs, and the general treatment plan with the religious counselor. And here again, a knowledge of some of the elements of psychology is important in the area of religious practice as it is for other aspects of care. If adults are going to serve children purposefully, from whatever point of view, then they must first understand them, as well as the meaning to them, of the experiences through which they have gone. The intense anger and hostility of many children in placement may manifest itself in a number of ways. There may be a defiance of adult authority, destruction of toys and materials, strong language, or other symptoms. In some instances, children use religion as a means of retaliation and rebellion. They are well aware that for certain staff members this may be a particularly vulnerable spot. If they can shock the staff member by profane language, refusal to attend services, or by the pretense of irreligion, heresy, or atheism, they delight in it. The important thing is for the adult to understand what lies beneath.

The director of one large public institution which tried to provide services for children of various denominations stressed the importance of trying to find young enthusiastic counselors. It is sometimes difficult to find enough leaders to come in from the outside, ministers and priests who are active with their own churches being unable to give the time on Sundays, when the institution is most likely to want them. This has sometimes resulted in the institution using leaders who have retired from active practice, and whose work, while appreciated, may not have the young zest, flexibility, acceptance, and dynamic leadership required for the particular challenge of this work.

In summary, the introduction, or continuation, of religious practice and belief as a part of the child's life comes not only with chapel, Sunday School, or church attendance, but also in a way of living. A growing faith in God flourishes much better in an atmosphere where trust in the adults around the boy or girl also grows.

12. Christmas

Before we consider the meaning which Christmas takes on for the child in the institution, let us look first at the child who lives with his parents securely in his own home and see what it means to him. His Christmases have usually assumed an established pattern. He knows how the coming Christmas will be, and that he can count on it. Every family prepares for and enjoys the holiday in its own special way; this the child likes. A youngster may look forward to going with mother to savor the department store toy display, writing Christmas cards, making small gifts, or purchasing and trimming the tree. Many of the same tree ornaments, familiar to the child as far back as he can remember, are lovingly unpacked, bringing the delight of rediscovery and the binding of this Christmas with those of the past.

Finally, there is the day itself, with just the members of the family present as gifts are opened, compared, relished. As to the gifts, these are an expression of love given to the child by those who know him well—his parents, brothers or sisters, grandparents, aunts and uncles. Family gifts are usually well planned, sometimes for months ahead, and are chosen with care to grant a wish, or as a surprise. Great pains are taken to find or to make just what the recipient would like. The gifts are intimate and personal.

The child in his own home enjoys not only the reassuring and known pattern of the preparation for and the enjoyment of this year's Christmas, but the continuity of all the Christmases of his life. Although family patterns vary, the way *his* family does it has the greatest meaning for him. He likes to have Christmas much the same year after year, just as the small child who has a story read to him wants it read exactly the same way, with no words changed or omitted.

In contrast to this picture, children in institutions may have spent their previous Christmases in a number of different places, for example, foster homes, relatives' homes, or other institutions. Brian, by the time he came to a children's Home at the age of six, had had eight foster care replacements and had spent each of his six Christmases in a new place. Many other children, like Brian, have missed the pleasure of anticipation of the repetition of a known pleasurable experience. Christmas time, which is a time when families gather closely together, brings home with renewed emphasis to the child in placement the sad fact that he is not with his own family. It is often a difficult time for him, this holiday which should bring joy to all children, and it happens all too frequently that the institution itself, together with well-meaning groups in the community who want to do something for the boys and girls, actually bring more hurt than pleasure. Such groups, in the kinds of occasions they somehow plan, without seeking help in the planning, often only add to the feeling which the child already has, of being different, of being away from his family, and of being dependent upon total strangers for gifts and support.

Let us consider several incidents which actually happened. In one city a group of neighborhood businessmen decided to put a box on the bar of a tavern, inviting cash deposits for an

"Orphans' Christmas Party." They then planned to hold the party on a Saturday afternoon in the show window of an automobile display firm, inviting the people from the community to come by and watch the "orphans" through the big window, where there would also be a sign telling that this party was being sponsored by this particular group of business organizations.

In another city a group of fifty or so children from a large public institution were invited to a party of married couples. Each child was assigned to a couple, who gave him a gift. As the child was introduced, it was with the words, "This is your mommy and daddy for this evening."

In yet another institution where fifty children lived, about thirty-five were able to spend Christmas day, or longer, in the homes of parents and relatives, leaving fifteen for whom such a plan was not possible. Those who were left were taken by a group strange to them to a hotel, also strange to them, for their Christmas dinner. Added to the reminder that they had no home to visit was the added jolt of being taken to the strangeness of an impersonal hotel, away from the place which was at least known, where much could have been done to make this dinner a festive one.

An elderly man, a leader in his community, asked if he might bring to an institution a magician to entertain the children for an evening during the holidays. The director saw no harm in this, and indeed, the children did enjoy the magician. But after the show, the sponsoring gentleman got up and made quite a speech, telling the children how grateful they should be to be living in this fine children's Home. This sermon was unplanned, and the director had not in any way anticipated it, for she would not have let it happen.

Each year, a department store in a large city invited to the store all of the children from the city's various institutions; in fact, buses were sent to collect them. The employees of the store were asked to volunteer two or three hours time on a Sunday afternoon for this occasion. On arrival the children were hurried through the toy department. "Keep moving, children, and don't touch anything." One could not watch the train go around, nor linger where special interests lay. Then upstairs to the clown, the Santa Claus, the little show, and finally, the small gift. The candy-filled red net stocking and beginner's paint-box, which a small boy might like well enough, only served to embarrass the sixteen-year-old. The nursery-type stuffed lamb, or the box of crayons added frustration to the occasion for the teen-age girl. (Too often people visualize all children in institutions as small children.) In the newspaper stories which appeared the day after this party, the boys and girls from "orphanages and other institutions" were described as dependent, needy, neglected, crippled, blind, deaf, and homeless. Youngsters do read the newspapers nowadays, as do their parents. An adolescent boy or girl, going out to high school, whose friends read these stories, has deep feelings and resentments about such accounts. At the conclusion of the department store party, a small boy in a wheelchair neatly summed up his feelings to one of the hosts when he announced, "I expect to be walking next year, and then I won't be coming to your party!"

What can we do to spare children experiences such as these just mentioned? Houseparents have often spoken of how tired and confused a group of children become, who may have been invited in a short space of time to six or seven parties. Often the invitation is accepted, the housemother is merely told to have the boys and girls ready at a certain time, and there is not even an opportunity to prepare them for the particular occasion; neither she nor the children know what to expect. But the houseparent observes the reaction, the increased fatigue and tension as Christmas approaches, and sometimes the destruction of impersonal and inappropriate toys received.

A child may become bored, indifferent, and resistant, attitudes which the institution can only blame itself for by allowing the practice of such occasions. The gifts which a child receives at an impersonal party, which may be presented by a complete stranger and marked "for a girl of twelve," has little meaning beyond the materialistic. A boy or girls wants and needs the gifts chosen for him and in tune with his own wishes and hopes. In a Christmas newsletter, Hathaway Home, Los Angeles, says, "Hathaway knows that lavish gifts, anonymous gifts, mass gifts, all gifts without personal relationship make the Hathaway child lonelier than ever. They subject him to the indignity of telling the public what he already knows—that he is less fortunate than others. They reinforce what he ought never to have believed, that things substitute for love. They teach him gratitude, not love. For he cannot love strangers, or crowds, or organizations. Nobody can."

The above statement indicates another negative aspect in connection with Christmas parties, which is the exposure of the child to so many people unknown to him. The youngster has already had a big adjustment to make when he came to the institution, with various staff members to keep straight, as well as all of the new children with whom he lives. He relates in one way or another to a variety of adults and children, and this is enough of a burden on him without adding numbers of other people who are bound to observe him and his reactions, and who in one way or another expect a certain response from him.

And now, what can be done? We must think, possibly, of proceeding forward on three fronts. First comes the matter of community interpretation, of teaching well-meaning groups why the kind of parties they have in mind are not what the children need, and which may, in fact, be definitely harmful. But at the same time, the interest and good intentions of such groups may be diverted into other kinds of help which are more acceptable. Second, the institution may need to strengthen, in a more thoughtful way, its own Christmas program, to make use of all of the positive potentials, in order that the child may experience the real meaning of Christmas. And third, with the help of the caseworker in the institution the visit of the child to his own family needs to be carefully worked out, both with the parent or parents, and with the child, using the strengths in the home situation but remembering also that a child's visit to his own home may in some cases be more of an upsetting than a happy experience. Let's take up these points one by one.

In regard to community interpretation, a director may explain to the representatives of the group who come with the party plans why such parties are not good for the children, and why this kind of activity is not what they need at Christmas time. It does happen that groups usually want to participate in a party so that they can see and be with the children. This is the part which is hard for them to relinquish. The staff member who talks with them needs to have other attractive substitutes in mind. How would the group like to purchase a corn-popper from which a cottage would get a year-round pleasure? Perhaps they might like to provide seats for a baseball game next summer? Wouldn't they like to buy some books or provide magazine subscriptions, which also would give

pleasure twelve months of the year? To give the institution a
check is also a fine thing, so that a housemother who knows
her children well can shop personally for them. It is a good
idea to have on hand lists of things which are not too difficult
for a group to shop for. (Shopping for individual children is
best left to the staff.) Such a list would include such items as
record players, records, toasters, corn-poppers, waffle irons, a
bicycle, tricycle, athletic equipment, ice skates, roller skates,
or a wading pool. Such lists call the attention of groups to all
four seasons, not just the Christmas period, and to the needs of
adolescents as well as younger boys and girls.

The institution which depends too much on outside activities often does not recognize the great possibilities of building
up its strengths from within the group life. What *are* some of
the things that can be done to strengthen the Christmas program from the inside? What can the cottage parents do to bring
to the child the deeper meaning of Christmas?

We must remind ourselves first that most children in institutions have not had warm, dependable, and positive experiences with their own families. And when they are able
to visit at home during the holidays for a day or longer, they
often go back to the troubled remnants of a family and not
to a solid reunion. Thus it is all the more important to remember that the way Christmas is planned for and celebrated
within the child's own group and with his houseparents may
be the first time that he encounters the real spirit of this
time, and it may make a deep and lasting impression on him.
And here is an opportunity, too, for cottage parents to do
something very special for the boys and girls in the group,
to share with them, to anticipate together, to prepare, an occasion both spiritual and pleasurable. Such a holiday spent

together brings members of the group, and the group and its leader, closer together. This should not be given away to strangers.

Boys and girls of all ages enjoy the small homey intimate aspects of Christmas. They like to paint the symbolic pictures of the holiday on the windows; they enjoy making decorations and fixing up the dormitory or cottage; they like to go to the lot where trees are sold, pick out their own, and trim it. They like to make small gifts, Christmas cards to send or take home, to have a hand in the baking of Christmas cookies, or making popcorn balls. All of this means doing, having a part in the preparation, putting one's self into it, having the fun of work-ing with pleasurable materials toward a common occasion; it means self expression. Children like *doing* and not having everything cut and dried and done for them. And it is only as the child has a real part in it himself, as he is involved, that it has the most meaning for him.

Christmas is also the time for learning carols and hymns, for enjoying this traditional music both by singing it, playing on instruments, as well as hearing it on records. The values of the good old-fashioned Christmas play are not to be over-looked, either. It is well if smaller children can hear the Christ-mas stories related by an adult directly, by their own house-parent, perhaps a student assisting with the group, or someone else on the staff close to them.

And now, let us consider the gifts which the boy or girl receives from the institution. To the child the gifts mean accept-ance and affection on the part of the staff and the institution. The gifts say to him, "We like you and want to give you some-thing that we know you really want and will enjoy." Thus it is important that the persons nearest him have had a real part in helping him to express his wish, in selecting the gifts for him, even if possible, wrapping them. Many institutions encourage the child to make a list in early November, or to write the traditional letter to Santa Claus. A boy or girl may make a long and extravagant list, which needs to be discussed with him by the cottage parent so that they can come to an agreement as to what is possible and practical as well as acceptable to the child. It may be that the director together with the staff decides upon a certain sum which indicates the amount available for expenditures for gifts for individuals.

Every boy and girl, including those who go home for the holidays, should receive gifts from the institution. Keeping in mind how important it is for the youngsters that we be fair, the gifts need to be fairly consistent in quality and in value. It is good when the child receives a number of gifts, individually wrapped and selected for him. This might include two larger gifts and an assortment of smaller ones.

At least one large gift should represent something pleasurable to play with, a real or a symbolic toy. For the younger child this can be a sizeable cuddle toy, doll, game, or wheel toy. The older boy likes construction sets, games, records, or a subscription to a sports or hobby magazine. The part of the adolescent girl which is trying hard to be grown up welcomes something which spells glamor, such as a new sweater, a lacy slip, or fancy bath preparations. The part of her which is still little girl may appreciate a doll or animal of the more sophisticated kind that teen-age girls like to put on their beds.

The second substantial gift which is usually popular is an article of clothing such as a robe, slippers, gloves, the particular kind of shirt or blouse which is the current rage, or a fancy belt.

The smaller gifts should include things which youngsters, particularly those who live in groups, like to have for their very own—fancy soap, cans or tubes of tooth powder or paste, hand lotion, hair oil, combs in cases, boxes of colored cleansing tissue, flashlights, and gadgety pencils; for smaller children— cut-out and coloring books, school scissors, paste, paper, scrap books (for *them* to paste things in), pencils. To supplement the child's main gifts, of which he likes to be sure, these smaller items bring in the element of surprise, of abundance, and also of delight with the experience that someone understood and remembered what this boy or that girl liked to have for his own.

A word might be said here about the relief houseparent. When there is a good assortment on hand of these welcome and usable little extras, it is suggested that the relief house- parent select and wrap them for each child in his or her par- ticular group. The relief houseparent faces many difficulties in stepping in when the regular staff member is off duty, and may have more headaches than positive times with the group. The work does not afford the same balance and variety of pleasurable occasions which the regular houseparent has. The relation- ship between relief worker and children can be enhanced a lit- tle at Christmas if it is made possible for the relief worker to give the youngsters personally selected, wrapped, and labeled gifts.

Preparation for Christmas needs to start far in advance in order that the gifts be right and personal. Christmas, if it is to be as we want it, cannot be left to chance, to last-minute plan- ning and uncertainty, and it cannot be dependent on hit-or- miss contributions which come in a week before the holiday.

Before the holidays almost any institution becomes the re- cipient of quantities of used, mended, and sometimes sadly broken toys; the question arises as to what to do with these. Sometimes a worn toy or article of clothing arrives deceptively wrapped in new paper and ribbons, labeled, for example, "for a boy of thirteen." The wary staff member has learned that he needs to be skeptical and to look at what is inside rather than trustingly include this package with a boy's other gifts. To give a boy or girl in an institution a used or mended toy, or a hand-me-down article of clothing, shouldn't happen today. In his life situation the child has already had to accept second-best in being denied parental love and the right to live in his own family home. The institution which allows strangers to give the youngster second- or third-rate used and unsuitable articles is usually rewarded by second-rate but understandable behavior, which often includes the destruction of these things. And we should want for him not second-best, but the best. Christmas time, as well as his birthday, should be the times for new toys or articles of clothing. It helps to achieve that feeling which we try to convey to the boy or girl in all ways, that we have a real respect for his worth as an individual.

To have a chance to shop and to see the stores is now a part of the Christmas program of most institutions. It is better when the cottage parent, the recreation worker, or someone else on the staff takes the group on such a jaunt rather than have this done by "outsiders." In some cases each child is given a small amount of money to add to his own possible modest savings so that he may select and purchase small gifts for whom he chooses. Children like to visit the toy departments of large stores, to see all the color and interest and excitement, to mingle with the crowds, but find that their money goes farther when they do their actual purchasing at Woolworths, Kresges, or other "five-and-dimes."

Some cottage parents are all too familiar with an overabundance of toys and activities materials at Christmas time and with a poverty of same throughout the rest of the year. This overabundance is not usually of the gifts selected and purchased for children individually, but rather of the more impersonal objects, such as small stuffed animals. These usually limp little objects remind us that there is not as yet enough general understanding of the fact that most youngsters in institutions today are of the preadolescent or adolescent age. There are, of course, also numbers of children between five or six and twelve, who do like and need cuddle toys, but a small child wants a good-sized animal, a thick, substantial, furry teddy bear, for instance, which he can take in his arms or drag about, take to bed with him, large enough to hang on to and to get some comfort from when he feels alone or unsure—a bear that will survive time and hard usage.

Whatever donations seem superfluous or inappropriate should not be distributed hit-or-miss just to be put into circulation. Those articles which have no point at all, as far as filling the institution's needs, should be sent to agencies which can make use of them (a children's hospital can use the small stuffed animals as counterpane toys). If they have a possible later use, they should be put away in a toy-storage cupboard to be drawn on throughout the rest of the year. Each cottage or dormitory unit should have such a reserve store of toys for times when there seems to be a dearth of play materials.

Christmas is a time which draws members of any family more closely together and this applies to the institution family as well. But even though there are festivities planned for all of the cottages and groups together, there should also be a smaller, closer, more intimate occasion planned within each

small group. Houseparents have spoken of the special value of
the Christmas that they and their own groups create together
—the small tree (even when there is a big, impressive tree in
some central place, the tree the child prefers is the one of his
own group, however modest it may be), the simple presents
exchanged, some of them perhaps made or bought with the
sort of understanding that only people who live together day
in and day out have of one another's ways, foibles, and wishes.
For example, Marcella loved sour foods, above all, sweet-sour
pickles, of which she could never get enough. As the girls in
her group unwrapped the small gifts their housemother had
prepared for them—combs, shampoo, and net nightcaps to
put on over the inevitable pin curls rolled up each night—each
girl found another small gift that could only have been meant
for her. The twinkle in the eyes, the look of understanding
which passed between Marcella and her housemother as the girl
opened a jar of sweet-sour pickles which she could have all
to herself—this particular moment could never have been
achieved, nor its spirit caught, by the giving of the most elaborate gift from a stranger.

It is in the group that the child *lives;* his houseparent is the
one who puts up with him when he is difficult, enjoys him
when he is in a good mood; together they share the ups and
downs of daily living, and together they should share this holiday to the fullest.

Some of the most sensitive and delicate planning called for
from the institution staff is in relation to a child's visit to his
own parents or relatives at Christmas time. Taking part are the
caseworker, the cottage parent, the boy or girl, and the parents. And behind them is the strength and solidity of the insti-

tution itself, and the well-thought-out plans of its own to offer as real a Christmas as possible to the child.

When considering the question of the child's going home to visit for a day, a week-end, or for the entire holiday period one must keep in mind the same factors that enter into the planning of other week-end visits home. Are there enough strengths in the child's own family so that the visit home will have some positive elements? The same basic problems which brought about the removal of the youngster from his own home and caused his placement will still be there when he visits. But it may happen, with casework help, that a family will try to marshall all its strengths, and concentrate its feelings of good will toward the child for the limited period when he is at home. It may also happen that out of their feelings of guilt over their own failure as parents that more than usual may be done for the child in a material way. But we must realize that in some families tensions, strains, and conflicts increase over a holiday period, and relief may be sought through drinking, quarreling, and arguments.

The important thing is to be aware of what environment, physical and emotional, the boy or girl is going home to, and whether the visit will do more harm than good. If the child has had casework or psychiatric treatment, and has experienced a more positive way of living in his group, he may have developed more insight into, and acceptance of, his own home situation which would make it possible for him to tolerate and not be too damaged by a visit to the home which was intolerable to him before. In other words, the visit home is made with certain safeguards and staff understanding of all factors involved, together with the child's own desire to visit, as well as his parents' request that he do so. For some youngsters, the best plan is for them to remain in the institution over the holidays. They may not be ready for a visit home; family conditions may not be suitable for a return, even for a day; and the best chances for a good Christmas may be in the place where a child's only, even though precarious, security is at the moment, and that is with his own group.

In some institutions the mistake has been made of allowing, yes, of even giving a push in the direction of, a general exodus of children and some staff over the holidays. There is a concentrated effort to "get every child out" to his own, or another, family home. There may be a general closing of the eyes and an unrealistic assumption on the part of both staff and children that somehow everything will be rosy at home, even if it was far from rosy before.

The boys and girls themselves feel that they must get on the bandwagon and somehow manage to get home. They become fearful of "losing face" with their peers if the visit home cannot be contrived. Many youngsters go through weeks of uncertainty, worry, irritability, and tension, waiting for word as to whether the visit home will materialize. And even when the arrangements are settled, they go through another period of anxiety about a last-minute break of promise, particularly if they have previously experienced broken promises, as many of them have.

Another sad fact is that this all-out movement at Christmas is sometimes given added momentum by cottage parents who would like to get away from the institution themselves, and for whom this is possible only if all the children in their groups are gone. Since a cottage parent must always give so much energy, time, and thought, and as a result, often feels drained, it is understandable that he would like to have the refreshment, the fulfillment, and change of spending this holiday with relatives in a family home. But these are the very days when he is most needed by those children who greatly depend on him and the group at this time. Even the child who goes home on a well-worked-out plan likes to feel that the houseparent is there holding the fort, in case he, the youngster, needs to make a hurried return to the institution, as does happen.

We have to be careful, too, that the boy or girl does not feel that he may as well go home because the cottage or dormitory will be an empty, lifeless place, that his regular cottage parent will be gone, and that there will be nothing to do if he remains. Such a child may leave to go to troubled parents who do not really want him, and to whom he does not particularly want to go. He is put in the position of choosing between two plans, neither of which is right for him. And this brings us to the point made earlier, that the boy or girl should feel a sense of real Christmas within the group and with his own houseparents, not only during the days preceding the holiday but at the time of the holiday itself. Rather than establish an "everybody out at Christmas" momentum, the institution should give the child the feeling that he is welcome to remain, that most of the staff strengths will be there, that everything is as usual, and that he in no way loses face by not going home.

Even when the plans for the visit home move forward fairly smoothly, the child's degree of anticipation and expectation of family love, of how it will be, are usually greater than the reality. He may return feeling let down and deflated, or he may be keyed up because old problems were reactivated in the old environment. The caseworker usually needs to be on the alert to help him with what has happened, and it is important that he not come back to a group which is limping along weakly on just a few cylinders, but rather, to a warm, familiar, supporting, and welcoming setting.

Frequently a cottage parent mentions that it is pleasant when there is just half of the regular group on hand over a holiday period. There can be a let-down of the regular routine, a later rising time, for example. The cottage parent can give each child more personal time and attention, and everyone is more relaxed and casual.

Sometimes the idea that every child should spend Christmas in a family home has lead an agency to place in foster homes, or with people who apply to take a child for the holiday, those boys and girls who have no homes of their own. Not many of us who are adults would want to spend a holiday with complete or partial strangers, and this is an exceedingly difficult adjustment for a child to make. It may serve only to add to his feelings of aloneness and of being different. And we must remember that individuals, however kindly they may be, do sometimes offer to take a child in an attempt to meet some need of their own, to fill an empty space in their own lives.

To the child who is sent away to the home of complete strangers, there is a triple burden. He already suffers because he has no people of his own, and his nearest relatives and perhaps previous foster homes have forgotten him. Second, he has the feeling that he must get out of the cottage, or wing, or dormitory, in one way or another, and so he feels rejected by the very people and the very place where his present security, however thin, lies. Finally, he has to pull all of his own resources together to make a go of it somehow in a strange home, where new demands are made on him for response and relationship. Christmas for such a child cannot be a very happy time, nor a time to be anticipated with pleasure the following year.

On the other hand, the caseworker may have found for the child with no family ties of his own a sort of week-end foster family, where he has visited a number of times before Christmas, and where he already feels relaxed and comfortable and thus would be going to a familiar place. Sometimes such preliminary visits lead to eventual placement in this foster home.

To summarize, there are certain holidays during the year, particularly Christmas and birthdays, when the anxieties that come from separation of children from parents are strongest. The child's parents feel guilty, and the child, too, feels guilty and upset. The houseparent, with so many things to get ready, together with the care of youngsters who are more tense and on edge than usual, feels pressed from many sides. Then, in addition, there come those groups or individuals from the community who are sometimes insistent on giving a party or presenting an elaborate gift to a children's Home which is not what the children need.

Out of all of these complications of feelings and emotions it becomes a real challenge to the institution to make this holiday period one which will help the child experience some of the spiritual meaning of Christmas. The institution is home to a certain number of youngsters each Christmas. The whole Home and the houseparents in each group can well place greater value on all that can be done, *from the inside,* to set the scene together with the children and to try to capture the real spirit of the day. There are wonderful possibilities in the simple everyday aspects of life and within the group setting which, when thoughtfully used, can provide for its members a more genuine Christmas.

13. Symptoms of Emotional Upset

One of the most encouraging developments in the institutional field is the increased recognition of the importance of the child's emotional life and needs. In the past the emphasis has been too often placed on the physical aspects of care, overlooking many of the psychological factors. There are a number of specialized institutions which state as their purpose the treatment of emotionally disturbed children and adolescents. But it is often said that *every* child in placement is, to a greater or lesser degree, emotionally upset.

Terms such as "emotionally disturbed" or "emotionally upset" are frequently and often rather loosely used today. The new houseparent may be somewhat confused by these phrases, not knowing quite what to expect from children so described. To persons not familiar with the reactions of children who have had an overwhelming number of upsetting life experiences, the youngsters as they are observed in the group may appear outwardly quite healthy, active, and normal. But the cottage parent who lives with the children, the teacher, the caseworker or groupworker who helps them, and the psychiatrist who may treat them individually or advise and direct others who take care of them, all of these workers see certain repeated symptoms and reactions which are associated with emotional disturbance. These symptoms indicate areas in which the child reacts too violently, or not at all; where he responds in unusual, even bizarre ways; where he is uncomfortable and not at peace with himself and the world. When a child is so described, he may have a number of symptoms, and in varying intensity. They show us that there is a deeper disturbance. Such emotional problems also hold back the child from growing, learning, and developing in a normal step-by-step way.

As we consider come of the symptoms which show us that a child is emotionally upset, the reader may think perhaps that many children in their own homes, with loving parents, may have similar difficulties. This is true, but with the child in his own home, one or two of these symptoms may bother him only for a while, for example during some phase of family life such as the arrival of a new baby upsetting the three-year-old. Or there may be one or another difficult period in the child's own growth, such as adolescence. But with boys and girls who have been separated from their own homes and placed else-where, any one child might have quite a number of symptoms and they are usually more extreme, showing deeper underlying pressures and difficulties. They are not so much a passing phase, and a child may be burdened by more of them and more persistently than is usual with a child living in a fairly normal home.

What are some of the things which might be said to char-acterize an emotionally upset child? It should be kept in mind always that these are not problems to be met head-on, and that we do not treat the symptoms. Rather we think of them as signs telling us that the child has deeper troubles with which he needs help. Nor is the list which follows a complete one. Emotional upset assumes a different form for different children; it is not one clearly defined condition.

1. Personal sense of failure. A feeling of lack of self-worth bothers many youngsters in institutions. They worry, "What is wrong with *me* that I am not loved or wanted by my parents the way other children are? Why did they put me away?" A child wonders why *his* parents quarrel, separate, divorce, drink excessively. He feels that they have let him down, betrayed him. But it usually finishes with the child blaming himself, feeling that he is in some way responsible. No matter how necessary or logical placement was from the parents' point of view the child still experiences some feeling of rejection because of the placement. The critical or angry feelings he may then have toward the parents cause him, in turn, to feel guilty and uneasy. Sometimes he behaves in such a way as to invite punishment in order to have the feelings of guilt relieved, momentarily at least. This feeling that the youngster has that he isn't any good because his parents did not keep him may show itself in an unwillingness to take part in activities, or to try something new. He may quickly respond with, "I can't do this," without even trying, convinced he will fail. Or he may quickly destroy something he has made, as no good.

2. Day dreaming, fantasy, inattentiveness. Most children, and adults too, do some day dreaming, but children in placement may be inclined to day dream a good deal. Because the child's real world has not been pleasant or satisfactory or happy, he makes up a much better dream world for himself, one that suits him better than reality. The child is often preoccupied with thoughts of his parents, wondering, worrying, building up glamorous fantasy, hoping for a visit, for gifts, but kept in suspense as to whether these things will materialize.

The secure child in his own home, on the other hand, takes his parents for granted, as children should, and may not spend too much time thinking about them. Dr. Bowlby * describes a small comparative study made in 1944 of 97 refugee children in homes in Switzerland, and 173 Swiss children of about the same age, eleven to seventeen years. "The refugee children were preoccupied with their suffering past or with grandiose ideas for the future. The Swiss children lived happily in the present which for the refugee children was either a vacuum or at least an unsatisfactory transition. Deprived of all the things which give life meaning, especially family and friends, they were possessed by a feeling of emptiness."

3. Impatience. In play and in games, in doing work assignments, the child's attention span may be short. He gives up easily, he is too quickly discouraged, or distracted. There is a restlessness, a wanting to move onto something else. When something new is promised, he wants it right away. He snatches at immediate pleasures and satisfactions. His experiences have taught him that promised pleasures are often not forthcoming, and so he wants things from the staff at once as evidence that promises will be kept. It is only gradually that he is able to wait with more faith for promised things or occasions. He needs to experience over and over again that promises are kept. In crafts he may not be able at first to complete even a small and simple object. He needs a good deal of adult help to complete a small task together with encouragement and recognition of the worthiness of his efforts.

4. Physical aches and pains. Any cottage parent is familiar with the many complaints which are brought to the adult's attention, of headaches, stomach aches, bowel-upsets, leg pains,

* Dr. John Bowlby, *Maternal Care and the Growth of Love* (New York, Pelican, 1953).

or just, "I don't feel good," when the child has no special place that hurts but does not feel well generally. A good many physical complaints have an emotional basis. For the child in the group, it may be a way of asking for care and attention that he would hesitate to reach out for otherwise. While he may complain of a headache, all of him wants to be relieved of the pain, and all of him wants the extra mothering and being fussed over which goes along with being ill and receiving nursing care.

An agency may have the rule that when a child complains of not feeling well, his temperature is taken, and if he has no fever, he is sent off to school. However, we must remember that the pain is real even when there appears to be no physical basis for it, and it may be a good thing for this youngster that he be allowed to stay home for a day or two. He might be in need of rest and sleep. It is sometimes difficult for a house-mother to decide whether or not to keep a child home from school. If she does so, then suddenly two or three others in the group may develop the same symptoms and they, too, think they cannot go to school that day. While on the one hand, the cottage parent or nurse wishes conscientiously to give care and consideration to all illness, still, on the other hand, one does not want too often to encourage a boy or girl to take this flight into illness. And here again, as in the case of many of the phases of practice, we look to see what can be done to make the child's total life more satisfactory. Other common physical symptoms of emotional upset may include sweaty, clammy cold hands and feet—signs of tension. Skin irritations such as acne or eczema may indicate a deeper underlying feeling of anger or irritation.

5. *The dawdling child.* There is, in almost every group, one

youngster who holds things up with his slowness, coming late to meals, being reminded all day long that he still has this or that which must be done. He takes five times as long as he should to get dressed, prolonging endlessly every move he makes, and often with a teasing, aggravating, air of "What is everybody getting so excited about?" While another child may show resistance by shouting, "I won't do it!" this slow child may be getting even too, by being annoying in his way, day after day, always making everyone wait for him, sometimes delaying the whole group, and getting a rise out of the adult who needs constantly to remind and urge him to hurry.

6. The hard shell. Some youngsters put up a wall, are hard to reach or get close to. Such a child holds off the cottage parent. He usually has had the experience that when you have been close to and affectionate with another person, that person may later hurt you. This is the way the child sometimes feels whose own interpretation of placement is that he has been pushed out of his own home, and perhaps in addition a number of foster homes. Later, he may have been in a temporary receiving center. Finally, in an institution, there may have been changes of cottage parents within his group. His emotional response is, "What is the use of getting attached to people, they only get rid of you or leave you anyway?" He finally thinks that no one will keep him and no one wants him. So he puts up a protective wall between himself and others; if he doesn't let them get close, then they cannot later hurt him by deserting him. A foster mother or cottage parent may give and give mothering and attention to such a child and may feel frustrated when he gives nothing back. However, behind the wall of the hard-to-reach boy or girl there may be an intense need for affection. It must be remembered that this need

is there and that the houseparent, the caseworker, and others
concerned with his care must continue to go out to this child.
Sometimes it takes years for such a youngster to again gain
confidence in adults to the point where he trusts them and the
hard shell begins to soften. This happens only after long periods
of positive experiences with adults and in the group.

7. *Poor school work.* This symptom is a common one with
many boys and girls in placement, including those of average
and above average intelligence. Often the child has moved frequently and attended a number of schools, thus having to break
off ties with teachers and missing the other advantages of going
through the same grade or high school without interruption. A
second factor has to do with the child's inability to apply himself,
to give himself wholeheartedly to learning. In order to learn,
the child's mind must be reasonably free from conflict and
anxiety, emotions which use up a child's energy and fill his
thoughts to such an extent that his preoccupation with his
problems stands in the way of learning and does not allow him
to use his intellect to the extent possible. He may be absorbed
in day dreaming and worry; or he may be restless and distractable. He finds it hard to sit still, to put his mind on his
work. Thus one finds children of normal or above normal intelligence doing mediocre or failing work in school.

Here is an area where the institution can give some specific
help both in providing a specialized kind of a school experience,
geared to the emotionally upset child, and also in giving individual tutoring. Sometimes a children's Home is located in a
community of an economic and social level above the average,
where a high standard of academic performance is expected of
the students, which a boy or girl from the institution cannot
attain. Or, his behavior may be too difficult or unusual to be

tolerated in such a school. While, on the one hand, it is considered good practice for those children who are able to do so to attend public schools in the community, there are some in almost every institution who have too many school and other problems to be able to make the grade. They need a specialized kind of a school with small classes, a teacher with unique skill and understanding, where each child has more individual help than is possible in most community schools, and where there are shorter periods of concentrated study, with more opportunities for moving about the classroom and doing a good bit of work with the hands as well as the head. There is a trend today on the part of institutions toward providing their own specialized classrooms for at least part of the children in residence. Study Hall, the practice of requiring all boys or girls above a certain age or school grade to study on their own for an hour or so, usually after the evening meal, is, in itself, not the answer to raising below-average school grades. Individuals in the group may need a skillful kind of tutoring, or at least, a good deal of individual help and the interest of someone able to be of real assistance. Often a youngster responds positively to this help and interest, given in order to help him to keep up with the daily work of his class, as well as to go back and give him a foundation of some of the basic work he may have missed earlier. In some cases it is necessary to provide tutoring in remedial reading; reading difficulties are often one of the results of emotional disturbance.

8. Enuresis. Bedwetting is one of the more common symptoms with which the troubled child is bothered, and one of the more stubborn, particularly for the child of grade-school age, although the symptom sometimes persists through high school. There are many possible reasons why a child is or becomes enuretic, and the basis is usually emotional rather than physical. There is the child whose bringing up was so hit-and-miss that no one bothered about his toilet training and who actually had no incentive toward a dry bed. With those children who have not grown emotionally beyond infancy in some areas, bed-wetting, together with soiling, might be just one of a number of babyish ways they cannot give up. Anny Katan mentions those "little children whose training has been completed by a beloved person from whom the child is now separated. After the loss of the love object, the child regresses, relinquishes the newly acquired developmental state and begins to wet again." * Bedwetting may be a form of protest, or of expressing anger not only against a person, but a situation as well. It may be one of the ways in which the child reacts to the very fact that he has been separated from his parents or another situation where he found security. As an example, Lucille, by the time she had reached the age of eleven, had experienced nine placements. As a small child her toilet training had been quite normal; there was no difficulty at all until she was removed from her third foster home which she liked and where she felt at home. In the fourth foster home, with a repressive and less warm foster mother with whom she was unhappy, she began both wetting and soiling and this persisted throughout the subsequent placements.

Dr. Margaret Gerard, in a study of a group of boys and girls who were enuretic found certain similarities in the cases. The boys were often passive, retiring, and self-depreciatory, avoiding physical activity and rough play. The boys were further described as slow and dawdling, demanding more than

* "Experience with Enuretics" from "*The Psychoanalytic Study of the Child,*" Vol. II (New York, International University Press, 1947).

the usual amount of help and reassurance in doing their tasks, easily distractable, inattentive, with school achievements below that of their capabilities. The girls appeared much more normal in their behavior. They were active, ambitious, some were leaders, independent and proficient in performing tasks. In play they had a strong competitive attitude toward boys. Both sexes shared a common anxiety, that of nocturnal fears. Quite a number had nightmares.*

The child may have a good deal of feeling about his bed-wetting, depending in part on how this was handled by those who took care of him before he came into the institution. He may have been shamed, punished, belittled, or made to feel that he and the odor about him, his clothing, or bed clothing was distasteful. He will be wondering how this new person, the houseparent, will react toward him, and what he may have to take from others in his group. If the adult has a negative reaction to the bedwetting, showing his distaste and impatience with it, the child usually cannot separate this from a feeling of rejection of himself.

It is important for the caseworker who arranges for the admission of the child to give the houseparent accurate information as to whether this child wets the bed and when this began; how the bedwetting has been handled previously; and whether the child wets regularly or only when there is a change or crisis in his life such as replacement.

When the child comes for his pre-placement visit, or, if the pre-placement visit is not possible, when he comes to stay, it is well if the houseparent makes some reassuring statement to the youngster. But it is not only the words which the adult

* Margaret Gerard, *The Emotionally Disturbed Child* (New York, Child Welfare League of America, 1956).

says, but the attitude of acceptance which the words convey. When the houseparent is showing the child where he will sleep, where he will put his clothing, and explaining other aspects of the routine to him, the adult may say, when alone with him, something along these lines: "I know that you have a little trouble with wetting the bed and I have (or have had) other boys (or girls) who are bothered this way, too. I have fixed your bed with a rubber sheet so the mattress will not get wet. In the morning I'll take your sheets and pajamas down to the laundry and give you some dry ones when you make your bed. As soon as you know your way around a little better, you will be taking your own sheets down, together with Jerry who goes down to the laundry each morning too." The attitude and tone of the houseparent, as well as his words, reassure the child that the people here take the bedwetting in their stride and in a matter-of-fact way and that it need not be anything which adds to his worries. Attention will not be called to it again, particularly in the presence of the other children. He will know that his meals will include the same amount of liquid as all the children have and will not need to worry that attention will be called to his symptoms at mealtime.

One of the questions which is often discussed and for which there is no clear-cut answer is whether to waken a child at night to take or send him to the bathroom to prevent his wetting the bed. What course of action to take depends upon a number of considerations. Like so many things, it depends on the relationship between the houseparent and the child, whether the child feels that he is awakened by someone whom he has known for some time, whom he feels likes him and wants to help him, and with whom he feels comfortable.

9. Running away. The boy or girl who runs away is not as

a rule doing so for fun; this is not a lighthearted playing hookey on a spring day. It is rather a way of trying to cope with inner tensions, to seek relief, being driven by the pressure or impulses over which the youngster has little control. While a child may run away from the institution after an unpleasant incident which he finds intolerable, there is usually a deeper underlying disturbance, and some seemingly trivial happening may propel him off. With some, the need to run away from home and from school has become a habit, which they continue after coming into the group, for a time at least. Or, a child may feel driven to go and see for himself what is happening at home.

The staff member needs to give a good deal of careful thought as to how the runaway is to be handled on his return. We should go easy in regard to punishment for this behavior. In many cases, when the disturbed child runs away and returns on his own or is brought back, he should be welcomed, fed, and reassured that the cottage parent was concerned about his welfare and whereabouts. One of the best illustrations of the turmoil which a boy goes through when he runs and runs is depicted in the film *The Quiet One.**

10. Hostility, derision, "toughness," strong language. This is one of the most difficult kinds of behavior to live with and to tolerate. It seems like such a personal attack, and the strong words which a boy or girl may shout out in anger or frustration, often carry intense feelings of sarcasm, hate, and defiance. We have to consider here that some of the terms and phrases that a youngster may use quite casually are ones he may have grown up with, at home or on the streets. They become a part

* Film Documents, Inc., in cooperation with Wiltwyck School (New York, 1948).

of his everyday vocabulary, and may not seem so strong to him as to a housemother. Strong language is also sometimes used in a show-off way, to impress others in the group who may admire and encourage the user. The kind of language heard often reveals an intensity of feeling which seems much too strong for the incident which provoked the words. Just a small brush with another boy or girl, a minor argument, a shove, words said in a teasing way will set off a blast of language whose violence is out of all proportion to the happening which provoked it. These biting and often obscene words show the seething feelings which lie beneath the surface. The thing for the houseparent to keep in mind is that the verbal hostility is usually not personally meant for him. He is there and happens to receive the full impact of it. It is important too that he not respond to the child with words that are angry or sarcastic, that the adult not meet hostility with more hostility.

11. Stealing. For boys and girls who have missed parental affection and family security, *things* are often sought as a substitute for the personal affection they crave and sometimes are taken also as revenge. On the part of younger children in an institution, the taking of things from one another is sometimes done by those who have had so little by way of toys and possessions that they simply take because they want it so much and it is right there, easy to appropriate. Part of the problem at this level can be met when the institution provides playthings for individuals, encourages the ownership of possessions as well as a place to keep them, together with an allowance with which to purchase other small things. Children who come into the group may have lived with large or small dishonesties, for example, the parent who tells the twelve-year-old child to say that he is eleven and thus be able to get into the movies or on a street car at half rate.

There is a more serious kind of stealing, which may already have brought the youngster to the attention of the court, and which represents a much deeper problem, needing special treatment and handling. When stealing points to a deep emotional disturbance, then the attitude toward it, in the cottage, is important as an understanding and sympathetic support, while the boy or girl is receiving the needed individual help.

12. The child who has given up. A child may have the attitude that nothing matters any more. He feels: "I don't care what happens, or what you do or say to me, what's the use?" Usually such a youngster has been deeply and seriously hurt so often that finally all the fight goes out of him, he becomes depressed, lifeless. This is a most serious kind of a situation. It is much better when the youngster is in some way struggling and fighting, actually trying to express and work out his conflict. The child who feels completely hopeless often needs special treatment from the psychiatrist, or the caseworker. But along with the individual treatment, he needs help too, in a small group where the daily processes of living go on in a warm and easy way, and where he has the reassurance that how he feels and what he does is important to the cottage parent, who continues to give out to him even when there is no response.

13. The destructive child. There will always be some children, who before they came into the group, and perhaps later during their stay, are destructive. This destruction may be turned on their own belongings, the toys of others, or group equipment and property. Such children may deliberately break windows, poke holes in the upholstery, kick the furniture, or cut up clothing. Destructiveness is another way by which anger, futility, and frustration are expressed, or empty aimless time is filled. Because of the events of his life, the child who is destructive may have a "what-do-I-care" attitude, or a "I'll-get-even, I'll-show-them" reaction. His seething feelings propel him to smash and break. In the institution this may continue, but with most children who have this symptom before admission, it does decrease when the child begins to realize that someone cares for him; when under careful supervision, he is kept from destroying property; when he is helped to have a verbal outlet, that is, a chance to air his feelings and receive help from the caseworker, groupworker, or other therapist with his real problem; and when there are activities offered such as football, boxing, or a punching bag toward which some of these aggressive feelings can be channelled and be given an acceptable outlet. When an institution finds that destruction of toys, furnishings, and equipment, or throwing, kicking, stamping on things is a major problem, it may well be possible that the total climate is not good and that the setting has added new frustrations to those with which the child came. For example, there may be more destruction when groups are too large, space too limited, where there are not enough planned vigorous activities together with sturdy equipment which offer an outlet for stored-up feelings and energies. If boys and girls have the impulse to get even with the institution for frustrations, restrictions, or unreasonable or unfair demands on them, and when there are not enough opportunities for satisfactory experiences, then they may react with destructiveness.

14. Temper tantrums. Temper tantrums are not unusual and they are another way a child seeks relief from overwhelming anger and frustration. The boy or girl may build up tension to the point where he has an outburst. Sometimes the incident which sets off a temper tantrum in the group may seem small compared with the intensity of the explosion which follows. Usually a child should not be punished for such a blow-up, and should be restrained physically if he is likely to hurt himself or another child, or to damage property. After he has been helped to calm down, he will, like a younger child, want reassurance and the feeling that he is still accepted and liked.

Usually there is more concern over the acting out, aggressive, destructive youngster who makes his presence and activities known to everyone than there is over the quiet withdrawn child who keeps all his troubles within himself—or tries to. Such a child may seem, almost, to have given up, which is much more serious than if he were fighting and struggling to work things out. When a youngster's feelings and expressions come out in an explosive manner he shows what is bothering him and his behavior often demands handling, as if he were saying *"Do* something about me!" Unfortunately the quiet child is often overlooked and allowed to drift along without an attempt being made to find out the emotional upset which lies beneath the surface of an outwardly calm facade, because he has pushed it down. Such a child is more difficult to reach and requires a special skill on the part of the caseworker, group-worker, or houseparent to help him express his real feelings, verbally or through play. Another one of the many advantages of a small group is that the houseparent has more time to give to the withdrawn child, to seek him out, to give him attention even when he has not asked for it and may appear to be unresponsive to it. When the groups are too large, the time and attention of the houseparents are so taken up by the more active, provocative children that the quiet one who causes no trouble is left perhaps to withdraw even farther into his own little shell. If a houseparent says "Oh he is no trouble at all," this does not mean that he, the child, has no troubles. It is better when a child can be helped soon after he has had experiences upsetting to him. If we keep him waiting, or if he keeps his troubles too much to himself, it will be much more difficult for him to be helped later. And without help his problems may grow deeper and more serious.

Other symptoms might be added to those already mentioned. Small children in institutions or hospitals show their great emotional needs and the lack in their lives of personal attention and mothering by head banging and bed rocking. If the fingernails of the children in any institution are observed, it would be likely in more than half the population that they would have been bitten, often to the quick. Some children twist and pull out their hair. Then there are always some boys and girls who overeat, seeking in food a satisfaction for the emotional void or feeling of emptiness which trouble them. One also sees the child with a defeated kind of tired posture. There is the restless sleeper and the child who has nightmares. In almost any group in an institution, there is a higher degree of nervous tension, of being keyed up, of hyperactivity, than found in a similar age group of youngsters living in their own homes.

Any houseparent is familiar with these symptoms which have been mentioned and could add others. Many of the children are heavily burdened emotionally with feelings of guilt, anxiety, failure, defeat, bitterness, and a sense of being in the way and unwanted. They have not had enough exposure to being loved and wanted, to success, approval, and belonging. When the negative emotions consume too much energy, they stand in the way of the growth and normal functioning of the child. But given surroundings which offer relationships with people who are warmly and helpfully concerned with him, together with opportunities for satisfactory experiences, we see again and again, that the child is able to pull out from under what may at first seem to be overwhelming problems, and to make a better go of it.

When we think of the factors which are responsible for the degree or seriousness of the child's disturbance it is important to know when the break-up of the home took place. If a youngster has had a fairly stable home life and at least one parent on whom he could count, and when his first separation and placement does not occur until after his sixth year or so, the chances are that he will be less disturbed than the child who experienced separation from his mother and placement in his infancy or pre-school years. We find many youngsters in institutions who have never known a settled security. While they may not have been placed until later, still the psychological stresses and strains in the home, leading to its final breakdown, may have affected the child negatively for many years before he was actually placed. And then we have many youngsters coming into group care today after a series of previous placements, in foster homes and other institutions. Thus a child may have experienced the separation trauma not once, but numbers of times. Each time the child is moved he experiences again the feeling that he has failed, that he has not been wanted or kept. With each re-placement his anxieties are not multiplied, but rather compounded.

Let's look at an actual group of boys between eleven and fourteen in an institution today, a group in which we see repeated many of the symptoms of emotional upset mentioned earlier—for example, the reading and school difficulties, enuresis, feeling of lack of self-worth, overeating, lack of purpose and initiative.

JAMES, twelve, the smallest in size, had violent temper tantrums which exploded about once a month and were at times so extreme that property and the physical safety of those around him were threatened. One of a large family of children who had been placed here and there, he was the one for whom there seemed to be no room when some of the others were returned home. Most of the time he was an alert, responsive, enthusiastic boy, good at sports, able to hold his own, but always tense and testy, so that he had to be skilfully handled, and firmly, but in a way so that some of the tantrums could be avoided. Too much teasing or friction with other group members could set him off.

RALPH, thirteen, was a sort of hill-billy boy who had grown up gypsy fashion, large, a tremendous eater, given to very tall stories of a boasting nature as to his own abilities, which were mostly talk and no actual achievement. He had a serious reading handicap and thus attended a special school, making slow progress. He had a good deal of charm, was a sort of ladies' man, but there was in general a lack of purpose and direction, and only lackadaisical interest in sports and activities other than as observer.

HANK, twelve, probably the most upset in the group, had been in an institution as an infant, then in a series of foster homes, and finally his present setting. The workers who had placed and re-placed Hank, thought they had done so carefully with good preparation for each move, but as Hank spoke of his former foster homes it was with the comment, "When I was *kicked out of* this or that home." Hank made pleasant, quick contacts with people whom he met for the first time, or casually. A nice-looking youngster, who might be described as a "regular boy," he had a real appeal and a way with adults. However, living with him in the group was another matter, for Hank was constantly into something, going along with any sub-group which might be in difficulties, or instigating trouble on his own. He seemed to be carrying on a fight against everyone and everything in an aggressive, persistent way. It was as if he was saying, "Nobody has ever stuck by me so far—I've had to fight my own way and I'll keep on fighting." Hank was at times the group clown, or again, the teaser, master of the wisecrack, aimed at taking the other fellow down, or getting a rise out of him. Strong physically, he loved to provoke a fight, being a match for almost any boy in the group. The housemother sincerely liked Hank, and he liked her, but she could not reach him to the extent of helping him make any real progress toward a better adjustment.

BEN came into care at thirteen following an unfortunate placement in an adoptive home whose expectations of him had been aimed much higher than his abilities to achieve the driving goals of the adoptive mother. He could not read at all, and even while of average intelligence, could not cope with the work in a regular school. He transferred to other women his life-long conflict with his foster mother, and resented direction from, or relationships with, women. He was untidy and disorganized as far as clothing went and a large eater, with a need for many in-between-time snacks and smokes. He had never taken part in boys' games and was afraid to. He was not accepted by the other boys in the group, and tried to buy his way in with them by giving them money or sweets, often stolen. He needed the support, control, and awareness of the cottage staff at all times. He had occasional periods of depression.

PAUL had lost his mother as an infant, and had lived sometimes with his father, and in various relatives' and foster homes. At thirteen, he never asserted himself. Overweight, heavy in appearance and manner, he clung to several of his infantile ways, of sucking his thumb at bedtime, wetting the bed, excessive masturbation, and attempts at mutual masturbation with another boy in the group. Paul felt inadequate at sports and in his give-and-take with the other boys, allowing himself to be pushed around. He was the butt of much teasing on the part of Ralph and Hank because of his babyish ways and immature physical sexual development.

AL, whose father was dead, and whose mother was in a mental hospital, was the largest and oldest of the group. He acted at times as a balance wheel, since he looked, and part of the time acted, solid and steady. Perhaps more was expected of him, because of his capable dependable appearance, than he was able to produce. If some of the younger boys made a plan to do something unacceptable, Al was inclined to go along with them. Anyone observing the group casually might think, "Here is the natural group leader," but it didn't always work out that way. It might be Hank, or James, who took the initiative (and usually not in the right direction) with Al following.

VICTOR, twelve, had been playing with dolls at ten, and for some time after coming into the group lived in a world of fantasy. He constantly repeated questions, not waiting for answers. He withdrew from and was resentful of the group as the members invaded his world of fantasy. Victor boasted unrealistically of his family situation. He resented attention given to others in the group and showed his strong feelings of antagonism. Though a good-looking boy, he was not clean about his person and sloppy with his clothing and belongings. He completely rejected any idea of helping with the cottage work. While of average intelligence, his school grades in all subjects were failing. He had spent his early years up to the time of placement in the care of three women relatives and thus desperately wanted a father and became unusually possessive of the attentions of the young man counselor of his group, and competitive with the other boys for this attention.

BOB. Though Bob was not placed until the age of eleven, he was even at three or four, trying to work out, in his own fashion, by running away, an escape from a home where there was an alcoholic father abusive of the four children, and a mother who had no affection for her family. At six Bob was swearing, smoking, a problem at school, and he had already come to the attention of the police for stealing and truancy, problems which he brought with him into placement. His facial expression was bland, neither sad nor happy, a denial of any of his real feelings. He was inclined to hang his head and sat or stood in a stooped position. It was a long time before he felt a part of the group and until he could be drawn into activities. Like Ben he began by trying to buy his way in, by stealing and giving things to the others.

JOE was a boy whose approach to life, at fifteen, was expressed by his favorite phrase, "Why should I?" He was described by the counselor as a boy with little motivation, for his dorm jobs, for activities, or for schoolwork. Repeating the seventh grade he asked, "Why should I study—they *have* to pass me." He resisted doing anything for anyone else. He showed little faith in adults, and a lack of conviction in anything he did. His walk was a shuffle; he seemed to have no purpose in getting up in the morning because he felt this day would be just the same as the day before. He complained often, "I'm tired." He was always willing to go to bed early and fell quickly into deep sleep, another form of withdrawal from his unhappy world. He was reluctantly drawn into playing baseball and every effort was made to encourage and stimulate a tentative interest and some ability in art.

MARTIN, twelve, the second oldest of six children, was least loved of all his brothers and sisters. His mother told him this, and also that he was bad, so he acted accordingly, carrying the air, "No one likes me, but I don't care." He was particularly abusive to the younger children in the family, and toward other smaller boys in the group toward whom he felt antagonistic as he did toward his siblings who were favored by his mother. His classroom behavior was difficult, also because of fighting. He did his homework accurately and with interest while in the group, but would tear it up and throw it away before arriving in the classroom. He had no close friends, was enuretic. The young man counselor of the group, recognizing Martin's great need for affection, won his confidence, gave him as much of his personal interest and attention as he could, and commented, "Toward adults in whom Martin does not have this confidence, he displays negative and unacceptable behavior most of the time."

The group was in the charge of an experienced housemother, and a young man counselor who assisted her and acted as the the relief worker. They had been helped by the caseworkers to be aware of the reasons behind the boys' behavior and reactions. For example, only one boy in the group, Paul, had a father who was in the picture, supporting him and visiting with some regularity. Ben's hostility was more readily understood when it was seen that it had been developing for thirteen years; James' temper tantrums were a bursting out when his feelings of irritation, frustration and tension reached a certain pitch; Ralph used his great proficiency as a boaster to boost his real feelings of lack of self-worth and his actual limited abilities; Paul on the one hand had a great need to feel adequate and able to compete with the other boys, but his fear of physical rough play stood in the way of accomplishment; Victor, who desperately wanted the father he'd never had, became possessive of the counselor's time and undivided attention. When one understands the reasons behind Joe's weary unwillingness to get up and face another new day, the enuresis of Martin and Paul, Martin's gesture of tearing up his homework ("I'm no good so what I do is no good either"), Hank's inability to make more than superficial relationships—then it becomes somewhat less difficult to live with and accept these things.

When we consider each one of these boys individually, all that he has missed by way of parental care and home life, when we see the symptoms of his particular emotional upset and the ways by which each one is trying to meet and to master some of his anxieties, we might wonder how the boys could possibly function in any positive way, as a group. For we have not only each individual boy and his set of needs, but the interaction and interplay of members of the group, which may be competitive, rivalrous, provocative, wearing, and filled with tension. But at other times a positive response and group loyalty is to be found, members banding together on an activity which takes them out of themselves, and having a good time together. Ten or twelve boys (or girls) like this can, and do, get along as a group. How they do, is another story, and one which unfortunately, has not been recorded often enough, in the form of on-going narrative records of the ups and downs, the activities and dynamics at work in living groups in a children's institution.

An attempt will be made, in the final small chapter, to mention some of the basic attitudes on the part of a staff which are helpful in working with groups such as the one just described, or with individual boys or girls such as June, whose story follows next.

14. The Story of June

The story of June, referred for institutional care as a "tough" teen-ager, illustrates some of the points about which we have been talking. The symptoms of emotional upset are clearly in evidence, and we will see how the simple processes of daily living were of help to her with their reassuring certainty. Despite a good deal of defiance, resistance, and testing of those about her, June was able to form a good relationship with her housemother and her relief housemother. She became interested in and took hold of some of the activities offered, experiencing through them enjoyment and a sense of accomplishment.

The case illustrates also how the roles of the caseworker and the housemother dovetailed and how they differed. The caseworker, in her conferences with June, was concerned with the girl's past experiences, helping her to clear up some of her conflict over what had happened before so that she could make a happier adaptation to the present. The housemother, working with June as one of a group of nine or ten girls, had the responsibility of handling the girl's present behavior, the realistic, current daily life of June here and now. And finally, in the group, June was exposed to a new concept of control, whose aim was to help rather than to punish. This was an important factor in her case, for, as we will see, June was afraid of her impulses to hurt other girls in her fights with them as

she had wanted to hurt her own sister. The story of this youngster illustrates that in some cases of children in placement,
the separation of siblings is necessary in order to help them.
We will begin June's story as her background was outlined by
the caseworker to the housemother.*

At the time of June's referral by the Children's Court, she
was being held in a detention home following a severe fight
with her sister Shirley during which a knife and razor blades
were reportedly flashed and both girls physically resisted their
mother. The Court already had a long record of the serious
neglect of the seven Johnson children, of whom June was the
fourth, and thus one of the middle ones. The father was dead,
and June had no pleasant or positive memories of him. She had
had almost continual conflict with both her mother and sister
during her entire lifetime, and at this time the girl was well
aware of the mother's rejection. Mrs. Johnson complained
strongly of her inability to control and manage Shirley and
June. The oldest son, Tony, was in the army. Two older sisters
lived at home and were employed in a factory, contributing
to the family income. The mother received social security
benefits for the four younger children. The two smallest, a
boy and a girl, were still manageable by the mother. The family had formerly lived in trailers but at this time lived in a
small two-bedroom house. The two oldest girls shared one
bedroom, and the mother and two younger children the other.
June and Shirley slept together on a couch in the living room,
which also served as a combination kitchen and dining room.

The caseworker's impression of the mother was that she
must have had a most deprived personal life herself in her
childhood and in her marriage. She was twenty-six when

* All names have been disguised.

June was born, and by that time she had already had four children. She seemed unable to see any of the needs of the two girls when they were discussed with her, and she felt almost desperate over her loss of control of the family. She was hoping that June and Shirley would be "reined in" by others and saw this as a punitive measure. They were the only two of her children she had thought of placing away from home, and her hope was that they be placed for a long time. As the least favored of her children, these two had been relegated to the least desirable sleeping quarters, and they had no place for keeping their clothes or other possessions. The mother felt she had encountered more difficulty in handling them than the others.

The two sisters had been running with a gang of boys and girls. Almost every evening they prowled back streets or hung around empty schoolyards or other deserted buildings. If one or two of the boys could get hold of cars or induce friends who had cars to take them riding, they played "chicken," a game of chase on the back roads, each car trying to force the other off the road. The girls and boys of the gang seemed to have little sexual interest in one another; in fact, June, with her jagged haircut and short jacket, seemed to want to look like a boy as well as to act like one. Mrs. Johnson complained that the girls stayed out late, could not get up in time for school, would not help her with the housework or do their own laundry, and were generally defiant and disrespectful. They were also stealing increasingly from stores in a large shopping center—mostly trinkets and cosmetics.

The caseworker from the staff of the institution had a talk with June at the detention home and described her as a large, rawboned, rather drab-looking girl. Her colorless dark-blonde hair was cut in an unbecoming fashion. One eye was crossed, giving her a somewhat vague look. Her posture was stooped. Her fingernails were torn or bitten down to the quick. June was concerned about her own plans for the future; her sister had already been sent to another institution, the Court deciding upon the advice of the psychiatrist who had made a study of both girls that their separation was indicated. June was able to say quite freely to the caseworker, "My mother doesn't want me. She's never wanted Shirley and she's never wanted me. She's tried for years to get us out. I don't know why she doesn't like me. Nobody likes me. I'd rather not go home because my mother doesn't want me, but I'd like to visit once in a while. If I go to the Oakwood Home can I see my mother sometimes?" She then asked a good many of the usual questions: Could her girl friends visit her? Were the other thirteen-year-olds in the seventh grade also? What time was bedtime? How many girls shared one room? What did the girls do? What kind of clothes did they wear? She said her own clothing wasn't very nice. When some mention was made of the pets, June commented, "Animals—that's the only ones I can get along with. Animals always like me. That's all that ever likes me and I like them too." When the caseworker, seeking for some expression of June's interests, asked her what she liked to do in her spare time, the response was, "I'm not very good at sports. I'm not much good at anything."

The worker thought that June, whose case history made her sound like a hard, defiant, tough girl, was really quite frightened over her entire situation. She showed real strengths in this preliminary visit in her ability to face her problem squarely—"my mother doesn't want me, she never did!" June showed further strength in being able to take on a plan of placement, to involve herself in it. She knew realistically that placement was necessary and she did not fight it. The psychiatric clinic found that June had good average intelligence. Her greatest needs, the clinic advised, were to be built up physically, to be made to feel physically secure, and to be helped to gain some ego strengths. She was to be helped to test herself out in a more normal setting so that she could gain confidence in herself.

In general, June needed positive relationships with adults, but at the time of her admission to the group, there were certain definite things which she needed from the housemother, and certain definite things she needed from the caseworker.

From the setting and from the housemother and relief housemother, she needed the physical security which the psychiatrist mentioned. This included a pattern of orderly living and a controlled environment. She not only needed clothing, but after it had been provided she needed to have the housemother teach her how to wash and iron her blouses and care for her sox and underthings. She needed help with bathing, grooming, and the care of her hair. The housemother expressed a consistent interest in her, in letting her feel accepted and liked. Various interests and activities were offered. In helping her improve her appearance, showing her how to dress, and reassuring her that it was fine to be a girl, as well as in offering a variety of opportunities for achievement, it was hoped that June would not have such a need to depreciate herself, and that gradually she would come to feel that she was good at something and that people *did* like her.

With the caseworker, June had regularly scheduled interviews each week—first, just to let the girl get acquainted with the worker. Later there were times when they talked about

what it meant when June wanted and at the same time did
not want to see her mother. The caseworker recognized the
bitter feelings June had in regard to the recent happenings
at home, and let the girl know that she understood how June
felt, her anger, her loneliness, sense of loss, and fear. As time
went on, and June spent some Sundays at home and then returned to talk it over, she had a chance for the first time to
stand back from the home situation, the parents, the brothers
and sisters, and look at all of it in another light—all with the
help of the caseworker. She recognized, perhaps, that her
mother did give her something when she was little; that her
mother had wanted to do for her and the large family, but
couldn't; that after her father's death, her mother had had it
all to do alone on extremely limited financial means and limited
maternal resources as well. When there were upsets in the
group (as was to be expected) the worker helped June to relate her past experiences to present behavior, as we will see a
little later.

And now let us consider the report of the housemother,
Miss G., on her observations and work with June, as well as
those of the relief housemother, who will be referred to as
Miss Paula. To help the reader visualize the housemother as
she discusses June, we might insert here that both Miss G. and
Miss Paula were in their early forties. Miss G. had had eleven
years of experience as housemother in two institutions, two
years with little boys, two with small girls, and the rest of the
time with adolescent girls. She was tall, well-built, had good
posture, good color, and a capable appearance. She had an
open, pleasant expression and a ready laugh. While by nature
a warm person, she could be firm and yet sustaining. She admitted that there were times when a group of adolescent girls

could drive one to distraction, but she liked girls of this age, and she liked being a housemother. Some of her other qualities emerge as we read her discussion of June in relation to the group, herself, and the relief housemother, such qualities as honesty, readiness to admit a mistake, patience, and humor.

"At first June was polite, but cold. Her attitude toward us was, 'Keep your distance.' She was somewhat resentful, distrustful of adults, slow about responding to suggestions. She resisted us at first, often using her favorite expression, 'I ain't a-gonna do it!' or going to bed and staying there, or running outside. June never looked upon either me or Miss Paula as a mother-figure. She had a mother and though she did not seem to care to see too much of her, she was there and no one could take her place. She looked upon each of us as an adult-to-child friend, as counselor and authority. Almost from the first she always checked with me on all of her activities, asking permission before going away from the house. Once she asked if she could go car riding (with some of her old friends of the 'chicken' game days) and seemed to accept it when I said no. I thought at the time she was really just testing me out to see what I would say.

"Both Miss Paula and I felt sorry for June because she was so unkempt looking when she first came. She was not liked by the rest of the girls and this gave us more reason to feel sympathetic. In fact, she was not too likable at first and almost made people want to draw away from her. But this feeling finally disappeared as June became more and more a part of the group. When she showed resistance, I think it was because she did not know what to expect. Her resistance was more against a situation or an occasion than a personal matter. This was in contrast to the girl who always says no when we say yes, just to take the opposite stand. When June stayed in bed instead of going to school I usually found that she had a special assignment which she did not understand or was afraid of. When she refused to iron after saying she knew how, I found the scorched clothing in her closet, and I did the good blouses for her while she practiced on the play blouses. Then there was no more fuss about ironing. When she learned to wash, there was less trouble on that score. If she could see the sense in the reasoning, then she would go along with us. But there was so little that June knew or had experienced, that she had to resist until she learned and believed. This was true in every phase of living—friendships, school, eating, cleanliness, work assignments, and play.

"Early in June's stay, I believe she felt my authority in protecting her, and this helped her to gain confidence in me as her housemother. I think that one of the things that helped her was that both Miss Paula and I stuck to our decisions; we didn't vacillate. We also worked together and could not be played against each other. I think that June was a little freer with the kidding of Miss Paula than with me, but she seemed to show both of us a good deal of respect. There was a warmth and humor in her kidding and it was her way of showing and asking for affection. June wanted affection, but not in the sense of an arm around the shoulder, or a squeeze. We felt that June realized our affection for her when we helped her fit a dress, set her hair, iron a blouse, or when we paid her a compliment. Sometimes June asked for these things. Occasionally, after she was in bed and the light was out, I would give her a kiss on the cheek or the forehead. She never resisted this and never turned away from it unless she was angry. At the time of June's birthday, Miss Paula sent her a birthday card more than a week ahead of time, and this pleased her. She kidded Paula about it but in the kidding we felt her relief at being remembered well in time. At Christmas time Miss Paula gave her a subscription to a movie magazine. She was thrilled with this and watched for her magazine each month. I made aprons for all the girls that Christmas, and June was very appreciative of the time and effort that went into this gift. Everything that was done for her, whether she asked for it or if it was done without asking, she was responsive to, whether it was shopping for the exact Christmas gifts she asked for, or the little surprises left at the bedside on holidays, or the blouse she found ironed, or the sox washed and put away in her dresser.

"June had been in my group for about eight months and was going along pretty well, with the usual ups and downs, when I had to go to the hospital and be away for a week. Paula could not be with the group as full-time worker during my absence but was to continue with her regular relief time. Mrs. Wirth, a housemother who came to Oakwood intermittently to help out, took over my group. All of the girls had been prepared well in advance for my absence and the reasons for it. Mrs. Wirth had never had an adolescent group before, and while pleasant and well meaning, she was perhaps not as firm, or as experienced, or sure of the routine, or as well acquainted with the girls, or they with her, as we would have liked. June was already jittery before I left, and during the week that I was gone, many of her old problems boiled up again. She had a physical fight with Karen, starting after Karen badgered and mimicked her. During the screaming and chasing that followed, June got her hand caught in the bathroom door and was hurt, but not badly. She had a temper tantrum while doing her kitchen chores because someone tried to hurry her, following which she refused to go to school.

"June could not accept last-minute changes. One day she refused to go to the dentist because he had asked her to come at an earlier time than she had planned. I tried to reason with her, to tell her it was a matter of convenience to the dentist, but she refused to accept this. I did tell her that she could not leave the grounds with her friend Peggy (a girl who lived in the neighborhood) as she wished because the dental appointment time was near. Peggy had been waiting to go out with her but didn't mind; in fact Peggy urged June to get ready for the dentist. She simply said, 'I ain't a-gonna go!' Again I tried to reason with her but she wouldn't listen, so I put my hand over the comic she was reading. She used some foul language and tried to get the book back. I held it so she couldn't see it. This angered her and without a word, she grabbed my thumb with her teeth and hung on. I kept my voice low and told her firmly to let go my thumb. I realized at once that I should not have done what I did with the comic book, because this provoked her into biting me, and I guess I was feeling more ashamed of myself than angry at June for the moment. She let go, went to her room, took her jacket and slammed out of the house. I saw Peggy take after her, and before June could leave the grounds, Peggy was standing looking up at her, shaking her finger, evidently laying down the law. June came back but would not go to the dentist—nor was she placed on the list until she asked to be. That evening she did not come to supper, but after we had finished she came to me and said, 'Miss G., what can I do with this skirt?' She said the pockets looked horrid on her big hips. I said 'Put it on, June, and I'll see what I can do.' This was June's way of apologizing. And that was the last of my real trouble with her.

"With me, and with the girls in the group, June was never a chatterer. When she did talk she usually had something to say. I had the impression that in her home they were not in the habit of talking things over. Some of the other girls, who may also have come from this type of home but who began, as younger girls, to have regular sessions with their case-workers, were freer in discussing their feelings, and in talking through a good many other personal things. This June had never had. At first it was only when she was angry or upset or when she shouted out a threat or accusation that some other girl was being unfair, that she could express her feelings, and this was probably the way it was at her home, too. But as time went on, June was able to talk more and more. She didn't have too much to say to me about her mother, but when she did mention her, it was in quite an affectionate way, as 'my Ma.' "

A helpful factor in the progress which this girl made was that she had the same housemothers, regular and relief, during her entire stay. Had there been one or more changes and broken relationships, June's progress would have been upset as it was when the housemother went to the hospital for a week, and there would no doubt have been regressions. June's disturbance at the time her housemother was hospitalized showed not only her dislike of change and any break in the routine which was beginning to give her security, but it also pointed up her fear that she would lose her housemother as she had lost her own mother. Another favorable factor was that the housemother and Miss Paula worked so closely and well together, and that there was no let-down when the regular

housemother was off-duty. They had much the same approach
and way of working. While the housemother describes her role
as that of a counselor or "adult-to-child-friend" relationship,
she actually did many motherly things for the girl, shopping
with her for clothes, for Christmas gifts, taking care of her in
many ways, and also representing a new kind of parental authority.

The housemother's story continues with a description of
June as a member of the group.

"June was a 'lone eagle' for quite some time. At first she
was not at all accepted either by her own group, nor at school,
and she carried an 'I-don't-care' attitude as she boasted about
her former friends and held many long telephone conversa-
tions with one or another of them each day. All this bragging
and telephoning did not help. It was almost as if June went
out of her way to prove that she was different and not acceptable to the other girls, as if to say that her whole background
is inferior and she will flaunt it. Later this interest in the West-
side youngsters began to die down as gradually she learned
the ways of the young people at Oakwood, and won their
approval and that of her classmates at school. She had an outside friend Peggy, and this was a rather surprising friendship.
Peggy was a small, direct, secure girl. Peggy often visited us
in the group and her home was open to June at all times. Peggy's
mother and I had a number of telephone talks, mostly about
plans for the things the two girls wanted to do together. I
think, through this friendship, June learned something of family living and home care. This was good since she needed to
know a good relationship between mother and daughter. But
possibly the friendship with Peggy, which meant that June

didn't have to depend entirely on the group, delayed the time it took her to become a member of the group.

"When June first came to the Oakwood Home, she seemed to feel that she was not up to the other girls, socially, intellectually, or in appearance, personality, and clothing. The attitude of the girls added to this. Paula and I were of the opinion that she was certainly equal to the others and superior in some ways to some of the girls. But she was not a real part of the group for quite some time. Gradually she won her place in the group and it seemed to me that this took place along the following lines: 1) Her own attempts to improve her appearance, washing and bathing more often and beginning to work with her hair; 2) Learning to give and take with the group. For example, when she first came, she sat directly in front of the television set, rocking. Gradually her chair would crawl closer and closer until she was within just a few inches of the screen. The other girls would complain, and when June was asked to move back because she was obstructing the view and doing harm to her eyes, she sometimes accepted the suggestion. But other times she would get angry, stomp to her room, slam the door, and go to bed, but usually she did not go to sleep until I had gone in to say good night. Later she became more considerate of the others' need to see; 3) Her absolute honesty. June was honest money-wise and in her own self-appraisal. One of her foremost criteria was that everything had to be fair; 4) Her generosity. She would loan anything she had even though it might be to the detriment of her own appearance, such as bobby pins or a fresh blouse. She was also generous with snacks she might have bought, or which were given out at TV times. She did not give these things in order to gain favor or the acceptance of the other girls.

"During the first six months, and possibly longer, June had a series of fights with others in the group, especially Pam and Karen. Both knew June's touchy spots and led into them. The first serious fight happened on one of my days off. June was playing ping-pong with another girl when Pam, standing on the sidelines, made a remark about her playing. There was evidently some name calling and suddenly Pam found herself on the floor with June on top of her, holding her by the throat. June seemed to realize suddenly what she could have done, for she released Pam and was upstairs by the time help came. She went to her room, flung a few pieces of clothing in her suit-case and ran off down the street. It was during the noon hour and someone from the office staff happened to meet her and persuaded her to come back, at least to see her caseworker, who fortunately was in and saw her at once and again after school."

In the office of the caseworker, June's first words were, "Somebody's going to get killed and I'm not staying here to see it. I'm leaving." She cried hard, complained of the girls taunting her, and not playing fairly, according to the rules. And if anyone called her a sissy, that's when she would really hurt somebody. "I really would," she said. "I'm going to hurt somebody. I just can't help it. I may kill somebody." As she talked further about the other girls getting her upset and mad and into trouble, she said, "Just like my sister Shirley." June's hostility, which had its roots in her lifelong conflict with Shirley, was being transferred to the other girls in the group. This hostility frightened June and when it became too great, as during the fight with Pam, she had to take flight from it. During the interviews which followed, the worker helped the girl express all of her fears and her feelings about what had happened, which she did quite freely and directly, the worker recognizing with her and accepting the fact that she felt this way, but emphasizing that June could not let it happen, that she would hurt another girl. In order to break the old pattern of behavior, part of the job of the caseworker was to use this incident and another, which happened later, to help June understand that the girls in the group were not Shirley. Also in this and subsequent interviews, the caseworker expressed confidence that June could control her aggressive impulses, and reassured her also that the staff would help her and would protect her as well as the other girls. Here was a girl almost desperately asking for control. The caseworker, in her record, notes here:

"In general, I have been trying to help her differentiate between relationships at home and at Oakwood, in regard to her firm expectation of hurt, rejection, attack. With her concern that she cannot control her aggression, as the fighting incidents have been talked over, I have helped her air the hurt she felt in the initial verbal attack, the rightness of her desire to protect herself, the appropriateness of her verbally expressing strong disapproval but the need for her to learn that she can control herself. With conviction I tell her she does have this ability."

The phrase "acting out behavior" is often used today, and here we have an example of it. Much of June's conflict had been over the rivalry and quarreling with her sister. Now she was having actual fights with the girls in the group. She was recreating in the new situation what happened in the old, endowing the new people with what she expected of the old, that they would act like members of her own family. She showed in her actions and told in her own words what was bothering her. But her impulses to hurt another girl were so real that she herself was frightened at the thought of what she might do. In her actions, June showed, too, that she felt she had to stand on her own, to fight for anything she got.

Some youngsters, with anxieties and conflicts over which they feel guilty, act out in this way in order to get punished for their behavior, and this eases the guilt to some extent— usually only temporarily. Acting out behavior is often very difficult for the houseparent. But from the standpoint of the child, we know more clearly what we have, and where he needs help. There is some meaning behind all behavior. As the youngster himself is trying to work his problems out through his actions, he gets response from those around him. It is his way of meeting his problem, but it is not a solution; the adult workers pick up the clues given and give him the help he needs. But the fact that his behavior, strenuous as it it, is out in the open is better than if he denies or represses it, thus not revealing in any way what his problem is. The case-worker and houseparent may then feel that they have no place to start, no opening wedge, and one hears, "Tony never ex-presses his feeling," or "It's as if Bruno put up a wall around himself," or "I wish I knew what went on in that crew-cut head of his," or "who would ever think that such a sweet, willing, polite little girl like Cindy would steal all those things?"

June's housemother had some pertinent things to say about the daily process of living.

"EATING. When June first came to us there were just a few foods she would eat, and she would not even try any others. Sometimes the sight of an unfamiliar food made her very angry and she would yell, 'I won't eat that——!' She ate wieners, hamburgers, boiled potatoes, and bread. She didn't drink milk. As far as we could find out, she had never had anything else to eat. Gradually by showing her how meat loaf was made and what went into it, we got her to try it, and after the first try she came back for more. Mashed potatoes, vegetables, other kinds of meats, desserts, were all tried a little at a time. She never hesitated to say she liked something after she had once tried it, even though she had declared at first that she didn't like it. In the beginning, in protest to one dish she might not like, she would eat hardly any of the meal. She liked being in the kitchen and helping the cook, who let her prepare vegetables, take walnuts out of the shells, etc.

"SLEEPING. When June was tired she went to bed. She didn't have to be told to go, or argued into it as the other girls did. Miss Paula had the feeling that she liked to go to bed because she didn't have this retreat at home, where sleeping conditions were so crowded. She was just as ready to get up unless she was in one of her 'I-ain't-a-gonna-do-it' moods. Then no amount of argument, scolding, or ordering her would change her. Toward the end of her stay, however, I think that once or twice we did get her up by reasoning with her.

"I thought that perhaps because of all the prowling around she used to do with her gang, she might want to continue to go out evenings, and would be restless and dissatisfied at home. This was not the case, however. She seemed quite ready to accept the fact that the girls of her age had movie privileges only on Friday or Saturday evenings; she usually went to the movies on Friday and was then content to stay home Saturday evening, or to visit Peggy, or have Peggy visit her. June first shared a two-bed room with a girl of her same age who constantly criticized her because of her awkwardness, lack of social grace, poise, and lack of interest in her clothes and personal appearance. It seemed best to move her into a room with Betty, who was one of the most settled girls in the group. June looked up to Betty as someone she admired and wanted to please. She was sensitive to Betty's changing moods toward her, responding with pleasure when Betty complimented her on her appearance, and covering her hurt feeling if ignored.

"Finally, after several of the older girls left, we were able to give June a single room. This was done in order to give her more privacy, some increased status, and a way to get away from a tense situation which might provoke another physical fight. However, after she had her own room, she showed no interest, as most of the girls do, in adding her own little touches, personal possessions and decorations, which make it their own. June's room remained bare and impersonal looking. (In a conference with the psychiatrist it was mentioned that this again showed June's feeling of lack of worth and her self-depreciation.) Even after she began to take interest in fixing up her room the only individual thing in it was the bulletin board, which was covered with pictures of movie stars.

"PERSONAL HYGIENE AND PHYSICAL CARE. At first June did not wash her hands or face except under duress. Later she grudgingly washed her lipstick off at bedtime, then later washed her face. As she became interested in new dresses she did a better job of keeping herself clean. She took showers, and sometimes enjoyed them; other times when she came out in a hurry in order to watch TV she looked just as grimy as when she went in. Lipstick was the only makeup she used, often to excess. The girls spent a good bit of time on their hair, liking the good shampoo preparations, and carefully winding up the ends at night so that it would look 'just so' for school the next day. Paula gave home permanents to the girls who wanted and needed them. June was subjected to a good deal of pressure from the group to do something about her hair. About the time that the girls began to accept her, they helped her set her hair and after a week or so, when she had done nothing to help herself on that score, they refused to do it for her any more. Finally June bought some bobby pins out of her allowance, and made her first attempt at setting the pin curls. It wasn't too good but the girls urged her on until she could do it as well as any of them. After the home perm which Paula gave her, she received many compliments on how nice her hair looked. She cut it all off again one night in a temper, but she let it grow, and the whole process was repeated, but successfully this time.

"June made a good weight gain and rounded out, having a nice figure which showed off to advantage with her better fitting, more feminine clothes. She had to have corrective shoes and the glasses which she had lost were replaced, but she didn't need to wear them all the time. In fact, her eyes didn't seem so noticeably crossed as they had at first. Her skin cleared of the acne which she had (and kept irritated by picking) when she first came, and when she kept it clean, it had a beautiful texture. The nails never did get a chance to grow out to a pretty length.

"CLOTHING. The outfit in which June arrived and insisted on wearing for the first few months was that of the times, and of her old gang, a long tight skirt, soiled head scarf, navy jacket, and dirty saddle shoes, with white sox rolled as low as possible. As she walked, her strides were long and heavy; we always recognized June by her walk, which somehow went with these clothes. At Easter I took her shopping and she picked out a dress that was very becoming and suitable for this rather boyish looking and acting girl. When the second Easter season came, and the girls were to get new dresses, some for confirmation, and some to wear for Easter and then later for graduation, June was among the latter. June would have been satisfied with just one dress, but without any questions or requests from her, I decided she should have a new dress for each occasion. When I told her she was delighted, and we went down to the shop for the new clothes. June was growing up and even her taste was becoming more feminine. Her graduation dress which she picked out, was very becoming, white, trimmed with red. The shoes were red flats, and didn't make her tower over her classmates as heels might have done. She was as well dressed as any girl in her class, and all of the clothes were of her own selection."

Not only in her sessions with the caseworker, but in her relationships with the group as well, June came to understand and experience that these girls were different from her sister Shirley. Even at the same time that sporadic fights occurred, the girls set June's hair in pin curls every night for a week in an earnest effort to help her look pretty. Her feeling of lack of self-worth improved to an extent, but still persisted into the second year in the group, as we saw when she asked for only one dress for her graduation, rather than two. Her lack of interest in her personal appearance and in feminine clothing stemmed from the fact that neither her mother nor older sisters took an interest in helping her. Also, if a girl grows up with a rejecting mother, she does not identify with the mother, who is a feminine figure. And another reason why June did not dress up was that the boys might not like her even if she did— she might fail anyway, so she continued to dress in an offhand way in order to guard herself against failure. The housemother was setting a new mother pattern as she took June shopping for dresses and to a "Teen Shop" set up especially by a large department store to properly fit adolescent girls with girdles, and particularly brassières, a phase of clothing and shopping very important to the girls in this group. The housemother, in helping June accept two new dresses instead of just one, was a giving person. Warm and maternal, too, was the housemother's concern and pride that June look as nice as the other girls in the public school graduating class. The housemother's account of daily life continues.

"WORK. June didn't like work any more than any other girl in the group. But at least she would go about a job assigned and get it done thoroughly if she felt in that mood, or half way if she felt lazy. In the kitchen she worked well with the group unless she was on with Janet, and then she would refuse entirely. Once after she had walked out, refusing to work with Janet, she came back to help me after I had stepped in to wipe the dishes, which was June's job. One time she quite spontaneously offered to help me sand and paint some furniture.

"INTERESTS. June played ping-pong pretty well. She tried hard and earnestly to learn to knit but was very clumsy with her hands. Her one hobby was collecting pictures of movie stars, and she spent some of her allowance money on movie magazines, most of which she shared with others who were interested. There was much swapping of special stars and comparison of collections. Her favorite actor was Jeff Chandler. She wasn't movie crazy but she did enjoy going to the movies, and went as often as her allowance allowed, about once in two weeks. June enjoyed listening to records and dancing with the other girls. She took swimming lessons at the Y.W.C.A. one whole term, and learned enough to enjoy swimming and looked forward to diving lessons next. She enjoyed volley ball and spent a good deal of time on the playground of the school, playing there with boys and girls, under the leadership of the playground supervisor. She was a real asset to the group in sports activities. June had done some ice skating when she lived at home, and this was an activity which she liked and worked on to improve. She received a pair of new ice skates to be used while at Oakwood, and was very proud of these. At the annual winter sports party she showed much spontaneous participation and interest. She skated most of the day, and was helpful to some of the younger children learning to skate. She practiced some figure skating and would like to go on with this interest. June did not avoid boys, but neither did she seek out friendships with them; she had no boy friend. She enjoyed playing with them at volley ball and skating, and toward the end of her stay, square dancing. I had been having a social evening once a week, usually on Thursdays, from 7:30 to 9:30. The boys from the older boys' cottage were routinely invited and the girls were free to ask boys and girls from school or the neighborhood. They could dance to records if they wanted to, and then I had card tables set up with various table games, as well as shuffleboard. The recreation room was large enough to have several activities of this kind going on at the same time. For one of these evenings, we planned a square dance. We had had one before and it proved so successful that the girls had asked for another one. Outside guests were invited. The afternoon of the dance June asked me, 'Do I *have* to go to the dance tonight?' Her 'No, I ain't a-gonna!' was discarded by this time. I said she would have to plan to go to the dance since there would be no one in her wing of the building. I wondered why she didn't want to go. After some lame excuses and hesitation, she said, 'I'll go if you will be the boy so I can be the girl. I may act like a boy and wear boy's clothes, *but I want to be a girl!*' This request stemmed from the fact that since June was large for her age, she had danced the boy's part at the last square dance since there were not enough boys to go around."

Remembering June's statement when she was first seen in the detention home that "I'm not good at anything," we can see the progress made when she wanted to take part and enjoy these various activities.

Through her accomplishments in swimming, skating, dancing, she felt she did well, and in this way her ego expanded and grew. And her own announcement that she wanted to be a girl was a decided step forward, too.

We have said nothing so far about June's contacts with her home and her mother, an important aspect of her adjustment. After the first rather long interview with Mrs. Johnson in her own home, the caseworker continued to work with her. Even while recognizing the mother's limitations, the caseworker still worked along with her in a friendly way, at first in regard to visiting arrangements. The mother was made to feel that she was important, a contributor rather than a competitor. In spite of June's bitter and freely expressed feelings of hostility toward her mother, she did rather wistfully want to maintain contacts with her home, and after her initial period of adjustment, arrangements were made for her to visit at home one Sunday each month, a plan which was acceptable to her and to her mother. June usually took the initiative in phoning her mother about once a week. With Shirley and June out of the home, and the two older sisters planning to move to a place of their own, the mother relaxed considerably, became more interested in working in her small garden, repainting the house, and taking sewing lessons, as well as participating in some church activity. As the mother became more settled, and June herself felt more comfortable, a much less hostile relationship developed between them. To ask a child to do all of the changing is putting too great a burden on him. If the child sees the parent putting something into this, too, it helps the child. The mother tended as time went on, to overevaluate June's progress and to think too soon of her return home.

June's story (which of necessity had to be greatly condensed, and much of interest omitted) draws to a close with a final excerpt from the caseworker's record.

"June's school adjustment has continued to improve, with much less resorting to staying home when at an impasse in a situation. However, when her teacher died suddenly and a new teacher arrived, June had some renewed difficulty in the classroom with occasional refusals to do a particular project. Once she swore at the teacher and was severely reprimanded. When June is criticized she feels extremely vulnerable and upset, and reacts with verbal retaliation and direct refusal to proceed about her business. June was much heartened by her improved grades and her teacher's evaluation of her mathe-

matical ability and verification of her good intelligence. While
June would have denied this a year ago, she accepted it at
this time and began eagerly looking forward to the academic
work of high school, whereas earlier she had figured on attending only until she was old enough to quit and go to a trade
school like her older sisters. Miss Paula remarked one day that
if she didn't know anything else about June's adjustment,
she would know from one remark of June's how far she had
come along. Miss Paula explained that when she first knew
June, the girl maintained that her goal in life would probably
be to be a 'gun moll'; now June was saying that she would like
very much to become a flight nurse some day, or a practical
nurse in the service, and that she would plan to get as much
schooling as possible in preparation for this. (Miss Paula had
been a practical nurse in the service a few years before.) June's
grades in school this past year were S's and F's, with one U in
Home Economics (satisfactory, fair, unsatisfactory). Sewing is
something which June has no interest in and little ability for.
She had difficulties in getting along with her sewing teacher,
and there was a great deal of conflict in that class. June completed the eighth grade with satisfactory grades. The results
of testing her for high school abilities revealed that her algebra
aptitude was very good, her vocabulary average, her visual
observation abilities above average, her reasoning above average, her accuracy in handling figures above average, and her
work fluency and expression below average. June was quite
pleased with this, and was quite aware that it was difficult for
her to express herself and be aggressive, in effect to expose
herself."

The case record continues with these comments on general
adjustment:

"It was after Christmas that there was real evidence that June's progress was somewhat more hopeful. She began to have a much more positive relationship with the other girls and with staff. Gradually she evidenced a good deal of spontaneity and initiative, participated more and took responsibility, and showed less resistance to new ideas, new activities. The housemother who worked closely with June, felt that their relationship was a constructive and helpful one. June pretty well trusted her housemother and at times of upset, Miss G. used the relationship to help with a difficult situation. This she had been unable to do in the past. June's explosive outbursts changed in quality and frequency, and she became more reasonable and willing to talk something out to gain understanding. There were periods when she felt under greater stress, and then she became demanding and urgent about her needs. When these were not met, she resorted briefly to verbal lashings and argument, but such outbursts gradually tapered off to a minimum. She always resisted attention to her physical needs, such as dental and medical care. She was always extremely sensitive to any need regarding physical care, and any illness of defect played into her feelings of lack of self-worth."

June had finally learned to trust people, but only those she had tested. The question might come up at this point as to her readiness to go back to her own home, which had improved, or into a foster home.

When a youngster has made progress, we have to remember that he may not be able to sustain, on the outside, the level of performance and improved behavior which he managed within his familiar group. When a child has struggled through a difficult year or longer, and his houseparent and he have worked together to a point where things are going fairly smoothly, he should be allowed to stay in this tried-and-true situation for a while to enjoy the life in which he has gained greater success and satisfaction. His staying will allow his improvement to jell, to deepen before he is ready to leave. Here he has close at hand, all of the support from his group, his houseparents, the caseworker, and others on the staff without which he is perhaps not yet able to manage.

After a year and a half, June did return to her own home, her mother requesting this, and June wanting it also. However, during her first months back home, June frequently took the long bus ride across the city to come back and visit her group and her housemother. Her interest seemed to be concentrated on seeing her own living unit and housemother. A youngster cannot make an abrupt break from one placement to another as he is sometimes expected to do. June needed to be sure she was not forgotten, wanting to see for herself if the people in the cottage were still her friends and still interested in her, as indeed she was assured they were.

It is often the case that when a child returns to his own home, or goes into a foster home, the expectations and hopes for the new plan may be much greater than the reality. The anticipation may be too intense and too rosy. This is what happened to June. Her return to her own home did not work out. However one of the first things to learn in child care work is to keep trying, and June's eventual placement in a foster home was a happy one.

15. Basic Attitudes

Houseparents bring to their work of child care, experiences from a wide variety of backgrounds. On any one staff there will be working together people from various related fields, with a mutual interest in children. But even when houseparents come from dissimilar backgrounds, there can be developed a unified attitude toward ways in which the needs of the children are taken care of. In this final chapter, a few of the ingredients of this basic attitude will be mentioned.

First there is a willingness to give, rather than withhold, from children already so deprived. This attitude of giving should permeate throughout the entire setting, including the staff, the executive, and the board. We give, first, the tangible things which any child needs—good food in abundance, clothing, toys, creative materials, allowances, pets, Christmas and birthday gifts. Second, we try to give as many as possible, of life's positive experiences, so necessary for growth and normal development, and all the more important for the children who come into care having had an overwhelming share of life's traumatic experiences. Third, a houseparent gives of herself or of himself, as one does in a relationship, of acceptance, warmth, humor, support, recognition, control, fairness, consistency, sincere concern, to mention only some of the many qualities needed by this demanding work, and which people have in varying degrees.

A second major attitude or quality is that of awareness, of observing, listening, of sensitivity to the feelings of the child, being tuned to what he is experiencing, emotionally. This awareness includes also the possible frustrations imposed on the boy or girl in this setting which is designed to help. One such frustration mentioned a number of times in the preceding chapters is the overly large group.

Third, we are developing more of a professional attitude, with the ever-growing appreciation of the importance of the job of the houseparent, and the body of knowledge necessary to do the work well. The professional attitude carries with it the recognition that the houseparent has much to give, not only to the children, but to the caseworker, the groupworker, the psychiatrist, and the administrator as well. The houseparent gives of his observations, his methods, techniques, and the answers he has found as he helps individual childern and keeps the group going in the right direction. All members of the staff recognize what the houseparent as a person means to the child whose previous experiences with adults may have been completely disillusioning ones, and who may again be tentatively trying to put his trust in another. A professional attitude also makes itself apparent as the houseparent and other members of the staff work together as a team.

A professional houseparent tries to meet the ups and downs of daily living, the rough hours and the crises, with dignity and presence without letting personal feelings get too much in the way. His abiding liking for children, together with the ability to take the long view (which often develops with successful experience) and to see beyond the immediate demand of the daily work, helps him to survive, somehow, the low periods, the drained-out, weary, "I-don't-know-if-I-can-take-it-any-longer" feeling that the houseparent inevitably struggles against from time to time.

And finally, a professional attitude carries the responsibility to keep on learning, through reading, writing, discussion, supervisory conferences, courses, as well as from the thoughtful observations and communication with the children themselves, and the recording of some of the latter. Such recordings would include observations of the child in the group, what he says, does, how he feels, how he reacts, his interests, in fact, all of his daily life in the group. Of interest too are the methods and techniques of the houseparent, and how he uses his relationship with the child in order to help him. Records of the processes of living, of the child in the group, and of the group itself and its dynamics, are much needed for teaching purposes as more and more courses for houseparents are being developed.

But records of this kind would have a number of values in addition to meeting teaching needs. The very process of recording sharpens one's mind in observation. The written material is useful for supervision and to show actual practice at a given period in the agency's history. The houseparent has a wealth of valuable information, too little of which has been recorded. It is hoped that a beginning will soon be made so that this heretofore largely unverbalized body of knowledge will be more freely recorded and shared with the wider field of child welfare.